ALAIN PROST
& PIERRE-FRANÇOIS ROUSSELOT
COMPETITION DRIVING

ALAIN PROST
& PIERRE-FRANÇOIS ROUSSELOT

COMPETITION DRIVING

HAZLETON PUBLISHING

PUBLISHER
Richard Poulter

EXECUTIVE PUBLISHER
Elizabeth Le Breton

PRODUCTION MANAGER
George Greenfield

HOUSE EDITOR
Peter Lovering

PRODUCTION ASSISTANT
Deirdre Fenney

First published in France as
Conduite en Compétition
© Éditions Robert Laffont, S.A., Paris, 1989

This English edition first published in 1990 by Hazleton
Publishing, 3 Richmond Hill, Richmond, Surrey TW10 6RE.

Translated by: Simon Arron with Chris Williams
Photography: Bernard Asset
Drawings: Véronique Sustrac
Design: Andréa Lebelle

ISBN: 0-905138-80-5

Printed in England by Richard Clay Ltd, Bungay, Suffolk.
Typeset by First Impression Graphics Ltd, Richmond, Surrey.

DISTRIBUTORS

UK & OTHER MARKETS
Osprey Publishing Limited
59 Grosvenor Street
London W1X 9DA

USA & CANADA
Motorbooks International
PO Box 2
729 Prospect Avenue
Osceola
Wisconsin 54020, USA

AUSTRALIA
**Technical Book & Magazine
Co. Pty**
289-299 Swanston Street
Melbourne
Victoria 3000

Universal Motor Publications
c/o Automoto Motoring
Bookshop
152-154 Clarence Street
Sydney 2000
New South Wales

NEW ZEALAND
David Bateman Ltd
'Golden Heights'
32-34 View Road
Glenfield
Auckland 10

CONTENTS

RACING ETIQUETTE

HOW TO BECOME A CHAMPION

PHYSICAL PREPARATION

FOREWORD

I have always thought it a pity that top-level motor sport should be as little known as it is. Despite what is generally seen on television or portrayed by the popular media, a race doesn't begin on a Friday morning and end on a Sunday afternoon.

There exists a side to motor racing which, although potentially accessible, the outsider never sees, a sort of behind-the-scenes world: the work of a driver between two races, or the never-ending pursuit of technical perfection, for example, or else the experience and knowledge that a driver must acquire if he is to reach the top of the ladder.

And should he succeed, his place there can never be taken for granted. Everything evolves constantly according to circumstances and events which might well escape the layman. But it's perhaps for this very reason that motor racing can be so exciting, even though at times difficult to grasp.

I've always thought it would be interesting to explain some of these unseen aspects of racing, and that's why I'm particularly glad of this opportunity to do just that.

I could have chosen to write this book alone, or else entrusted the job to a third party. However, I have preferred to share the task with Pierre-François Rousselot, a highly experienced and active driver, as well as an accomplished journalist. More importantly, he and I are on the same wavelength ... in short, he has been the ideal partner in this project.

Alain Prost

Pierre-François Rousselot is one of the few motoring journalists to have practised top-level motor sport, and he has a deep knowledge of his subject: for ten years he was an instructor and later director of the racing school at Magny-Cours, from which several future F1 stars have graduated.

Moreover, he contested over 100 single-seater races, pipping the late Patrick Depailler to the European F3 title in 1971. In 1988, in his tenth Le Mans, he collected the award for the highest-placed French finisher. Some 15 years as a journalist and test driver have allowed 'P.F.R.' to sample many of the world's most powerful competition cars.

FOREWORD

I f I have learnt one thing from ten years of imparting the art of racing driving to budding champions at Magny-Cours in France, it must be the appreciation that this is a subject far too rich and complex to teach solely according to the traditional method of nebulous theories and physical laws.

To pompous, incomprehensible theses, I have always preferred simple explanations, concrete descriptions and realistic examples.

My desire for clarity and simplicity has led me to divide this exciting subject into logical, sequential categories: the basic techniques of driving a racing car; testing and chassis development; and, finally, what is expected of a driver in the big, wide world of motor sport. To conclude, I have reflected on how one becomes a successful racing driver and what magic spark turns a good driver into a world-beating champion.

In preparing what follows, I have endeavoured to include all the information and hints that I, as a youngster, would have loved to have found when I too dreamed of becoming a racing driver.

Alain Prost's invaluable contribution is an endorsement of this book's quality and accuracy which will escape no one. Alain, a long-standing friend, wished to do more than simply write an honorary foreword. Instead, this champion among champions insisted on making his personal contribution to each chapter, combining his inestimable experience with the observations and advice of a true pro.

For his valued assistance, I take this opportunity to offer him my sincerest thanks.

Pierre-François Rousselot

DRIVING
TECHNIQUES

DRIVING POSITION

As is traditional in any book concerning driving techniques, it is best to start by making the driver comfortable in his car.

To begin with, you must take into account both the relationship between arms, hands and steering wheel, and that between legs, feet and the car's pedals. These relationships are crucial to driving efficiency.

In competition, any number of adjustments are available. You must aim to find the best seating position so that all movements can be made as freely as possible. You should not end up fully stretched; conversely, you must rule out anything which puts too much constraint on the body. That leads to discomfort, fatigue and probable cramp.

In concrete terms, by the end of a race the left leg should never be too tense from declutching, nor the right (particularly the **knee** and ankle) too stiff from continual acceleration and braking.

■ The steering wheel

The same considerations apply to the upper body. Arms should never be fully extended in order to reach the wheel, nor should elbows be so far bent that they are jammed into your chest. It has often been said that there is an ideal angle and distance at which the arms should be placed. In truth, it is impossible to make such a generalisation. Everyone comes into motor racing with a shape all of their own. Some drivers have long legs, others have short arms; all succeed in finding a suitable compromise in order to be completely relaxed in their car.

But there are still a few basic guidelines. Thus you must be able to make a complete turn of the wheel without either getting stuck or lifting your shoulders away from the seat. Also, your arm should never be fully stretched when you place a hand on top of the steering wheel – the furthest point from the body given the angle at which it is raked.

The steering wheel of a racing car is generally adjustable for both height and reach. For several years, the tendency has been to place it as high as possible. This has two practical benefits:

– there is more free space between the top of the thighs, pelvis and arms;
– with the wheel in this position, hands and forearms can be used to best effect.

This point shouldn't be overlooked. Racing cars seldom have power-assisted steering; they are relatively cumbersome and heavy, hence the advantage of placing the wheel in a position that eases and relieves muscular exertion. Racing demands an ability to turn the wheel frequently, from one bend to the next, and always with speed, precision and sensitivity. So you see why it is essential that there should be no unnecessarily awkward movements. If such and

such a champion prefers to lean forward with his chest close to the wheel, that's no reason to follow his example. For him, it is a way of being comfortable. It is up to each individual to arrange his cockpit so that arms and legs are unimpeded for maximum efficiency.

Avoid these two extremes as far as driving position is concerned. In the top picture, the driver is too far from the wheel. His arms are too stretched and have little margin for manoeuvring. In the second example, the driver is too close. His arms are totally bent and freedom of movement is excessively restricted.

■ The footrest

In a racing car, it is imperative that the left leg should be firmly supported. To this end, there is usually a fourth 'pedal', to the left of the clutch and at the same height, which acts as a footrest. This is a vital point. Having declutched, the left leg should not rest inert. Placing it on the footrest helps a driver to wedge himself more firmly in place.

■ The seat

A racing seat isn't simply something for sitting on. It should fit as snugly as possible, and the further you progress up the motor racing ladder, the more you'll find seats that are specifically moulded around individual drivers. Alain Prost, for instance, thinks nothing of spending several days trying out and perfecting his own.

The driver sits in his own preferred driving position, and a variety of hot foam compounds are poured around him to create a mould which fits his body exactly. Installed in one of these, the driver is held firmly in place. He feels at one with the car, and

in a way becomes an extension of it. He feels everything it does and notices every response, from the slightest vibration to a violent loss of adhesion.

The footrest supports the left leg, the seat ensconces the body and the six-point safety harness, apart from its obvious role, grips chest and pelvis. These installations are intended to hold the driver firmly in place in order to permit maximum driving precision.

At a certain level of racing, it is important for a driver to have his own personal seat. Moulded around his body, it allows him to be totally at one with the car, enabling him to perceive even the slightest reactions of the chassis.

HANDS ON
THE WHEEL

In a straight line, when a driver is in perfect control, the hands should be diametrically opposite each other on the wheel, and in a horizontal plane. If you imagine the wheel as a clock face, the driver's hands would indicate a quarter to three. In theory that is the ideal position. The wheel should be held firmly so that the car doesn't break away, but the hands should on no account be too tense or too close. If the body is well supported elsewhere, there should be no need for the driver to cling to the wheel. It allows you both control of and a feel for the car: it turns the front wheels, of course, but it also transmits various responses (vibrations, slides, lock-ups). An ill-positioned driver, sliding around in corners and clutching at the wheel, will be depriving himself of a source of basic information. In effect, he will be incapable of anticipating the car's reactions, a vital aspect of driving efficiency.

Generally, a racing car (single-seater or sports car) has very precise steering: from lock to lock, there is usually only one turn of the wheel, a turn and a half at most. On less specialised racers (such as saloons and rally cars), there will perhaps be three turns lock to lock: one and a half to the left, and the same to the right.

In the former, the driver barely has to move his hands on the wheel. To take a right turn at the end of a straight, you should keep your hands at a quarter to three. The left hand does the work, easing the car onto the racing line. The right will do its bit simply by staying put on the wheel.

At the exit of the corner, to straighten the wheels, the reverse applies: the right hand initiates the manoeuvre, assisted

1

2

4

5

by the left. The hands should never slide around the wheel, and should always remain in the same position on the wheel, no matter what type of corner you are tackling (fast curves, tight bends or hairpins). A single-seater driver can thus complete a full lap without shifting his hands on the wheel.

In the case of cars with less direct steering, the driver adopts a markedly different driving style. Given that you might need to make more than a complete turn of the wheel, the hands should not be kept in a fixed position. You can imagine the adverse effect of reducing the possible angles of lock and opposite lock on the front wheels. With this type of steering, the driver should feed the wheel through his fingers to ensure

Alain Prost: 'Along a straight, my arms would be relatively crooked so as not to become too straight while cornering (1). Moving down the gears under braking, only my left hand controls the car (2).

'Lock to lock on a Formula 1 car requires just one full turn of the steering wheel, so I never have to take my hands off it except to change gear. The next sequence of photos shows hand positions in different circumstances: entering a fast right-hander (3); opposite-locking in the same corner (4); entering a very tight hairpin-right (5); and opposite-locking out of the same hairpin (6). Picture 6 might also illustrate steering correction through a medium-speed bend in the wet.'

perfect control. In principle, it is best to keep the hands as far apart as possible, ideally opposite each other, so that each retains maximum efficiency.

In practice, putting theory aside for a moment, the speed and precision of steering inputs are vital if you want to be a good driver. It is one hundred times better to make accurate steering corrections with your arms in an untidy jumble than to make poorly timed movements with your hands in a perfect position. There are often situations which demand urgent attention, for instance when you change down too late and your right hand is still on the gear lever as you reach the entry to a left-hand bend...

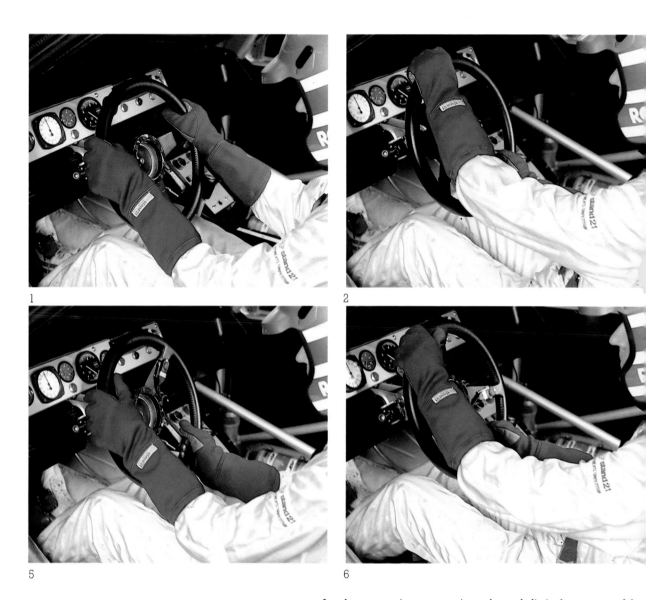

1

2

5

6

In saloon car racing, on occasions when only limited movement of the steering wheel is required, hand positions are the same as those for a single-seater: along a straight (1); a right-hand bend (2); and opposite-locking (3).

For slower, tighter corners, however, since lock to lock requires something like three full revolutions of the steering wheel, it is important to position the hands in anticipation. For a 90-degree right-hander, for example, the right hand collects the wheel at 12 o'clock (4), then turns it by a good half-turn (5). The left hand initially lets the wheel slip through its grip, then takes a firm hold, continuing the movement in order to

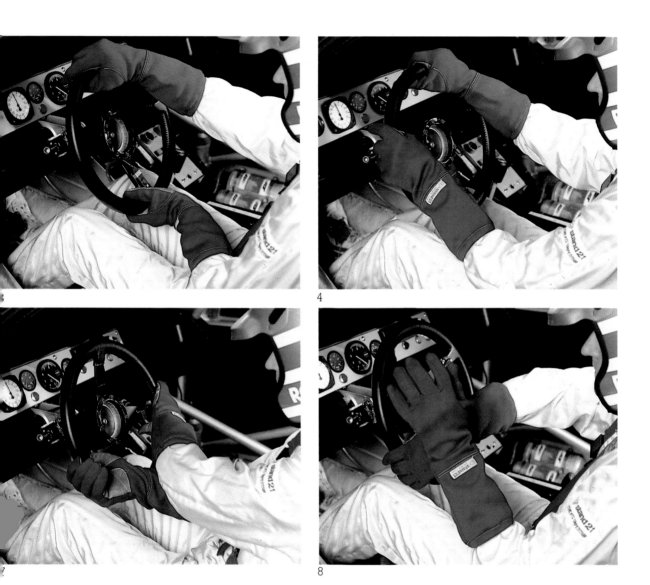

3

4

7

8

make any necessary corrections through the corner (6). For an extremely tight hairpin, the left hand could continue for a further third of a turn (7), which effectively means the wheel has carried out nearly one full revolution to the right. A further situation where hands might come off the steering wheel would be when applying a great deal of opposite lock, coming out of a hairpin in the wet, for example. In which case, the left hand moves clear in order to allow the right hand total freedom of movement (8).

This sequence was shot inside the 4WD Renault 21 Turbo which Jean Ragnotti took to the French production car title in 1988.

MAKING THE MOST
OF YOUR BRAKES

In normal driving conditions, even at speed, whether on urban roads or motorways, you are considered a good driver if you don't brake fiercely. Basically, anticipating what's going on around you, not being rough with the car and not upsetting your passengers by braking violently are essential qualities for good driving. But in racing, everything is quite the opposite. The driver tries to keep his foot hard down for as long as possible. On reaching a corner, you wait until the last possible moment before stamping on the brakes. In racing, you brake as hard as you can over the shortest possible distance.

The object of braking is to slow the car down to the perfect speed for entry into a corner. The braking distance varies according to how much you need to slow down. In extreme circumstances, at Le Mans for example, drivers sped through Hunaudières at 225 mph on the old straight before dropping to around 40 mph for Mulsanne Corner. But no matter which situation you consider, the principle always remains the same: brake as hard and as late as possible. In character, braking in a race is completely opposite to that in everyday driving: it is normal for a racing driver to brake as might Joe Public when suddenly confronted by an unseen danger. That is the best way to describe it.

I know from experience that this is a delicate part of the learning process. So different is it to normal road behaviour that beginners don't always adapt.

When you lift your foot from the accelerator, you do so to apply it to the brakes as quickly as possible. Racing jargon is explicit on this point: you 'jump' from one pedal to the other, and you

always press hard.

You might detect here a hint of brutality. In reality, racing demands that a driver's actions are precise, sensitive and very fast. The explanation is simple: moving slowly from one pedal to the other increases the length of time during which the car is neither at full acceleration nor full deceleration. Whether you are switching from the throttle to the

brake or vice versa, any delay will have the same effect: loss of time.

There is a second point worthy of mention. Braking systems on racing cars rarely benefit from power assistance. There are no concessions to comfort, and you mustn't expect to find the smoothness you get with servo-assisted brakes in production cars. Braking thus demands an important muscular effort.

Before the Le Mans 24 Hours circuit was modified at the start of 1990, braking for Mulsanne at the end of the Hunaudières Straight saw Group C cars decelerate by nearly 190 mph in just 300 yards! In this sort of situation, braking must be relatively progressive in order for the transfer of weight to the front wheels to be as gradual as possible.

Gilles Villeneuve locks the wheels of his Ferrari T3 at Zolder in 1979. Entry into the ensuing tight corner is very quick and heavy braking is called for. The Canadian driver has already started to steer right.

■ Locking wheels

The need to brake so hard creates an extra difficulty, critical in racing, namely the need to avoid locking up wheels. It can happen to one, two or indeed all four, and not necessarily simultaneously.

If you lock up a rear wheel, its level of grip is immediately reduced, as is overall braking efficiency.

If it happens to a front wheel, the consequences can be more serious:

– deceleration is even less effective;
– you lose all steering control no matter how you turn the wheel.

Generally speaking, a locked

wheel will henceforth be of no use.

You will soon discover that this momentary lapse has taken a more serious toll: a locked wheel provokes excessive tyre wear at the point where the rubber is in contact with the track surface.

That is particularly true when the tyres are made of a soft rubber compound. They are produced for a specific purpose, and have a short lifespan to start with. Certain soft tyres are designed to last for just two or three laps; other harder compounds might last for 300 miles at the most.

When a soft-compound tyre locks up, the friction is such that it produces what we call a 'flat spot', and thus the tyre's perfect round shape is ruined.

Down the following straight, the driver will feel violent jolts: the tyre is out of balance! The wheel's lead balancing weights aren't to blame, and are doing their job as usual. But a vital strip of rubber has been shaved from the tyre, and this loss of weight, amplified by the high speed at which the wheel rotates, provokes such sharp vibrations through the steering wheel that it can become impossible to steer and control the car.

Remember too that a tyre which already has a flat spot tends to lock up at the same place at the next braking point. You thus enter a vicious circle and it's up to the driver to be aware of the situation very quickly. Such awareness is a matter of sensitivity and 'feel'. This is something that theory alone cannot satisfactorily convey.

A good driver is one who brakes hard, yet with sufficient sensitivity to detect the first signs of lock-up through the pedal. Sensitive judgement is required to tread gently enough on the pedal to avoid making this mistake, while at the same time doing so hard enough to slow the car sufficiently...

Furthermore, the driver must fine-tune his senses to pin-point the lock-up, such are the number of possible eventualities: front-left wheel and/or front-right wheel, both right-hand/left-hand wheels, and so on. You can't see the wheel concerned, so everything has to be detected by feel.

The old braking chestnut 'stamp hard, back off, reapply pressure' is a simplistic formula without any deep theoretical basis. There is no way of proving that the point at which you release the pedal is appropriate; on the contrary, it might be better to brake even harder at that precise moment.

Another notion from a bygone age concerns drivers' frequent preoccupation with overheating the brakes through overuse. Technical advances have solved this problem: nowadays racing and rally cars are, with precious few exceptions, equipped to cope with braking demands for the duration of an event.

■ Perfect braking

Technically speaking, perfect braking is extremely difficult to achieve.

It's a motor racing tradition to go and see the competition in action. You learn a lot from watching your opposition, whether about the technical ability of rival drivers or about the behaviour of their cars. From the side of the track, the trained eye of a racing driver can immediately identify ideal use of the brakes.

It is clearly impossible to see precisely what is happening to the wheels of a car travelling at speed. On the other hand, you should be able to spot, in a braking area, the smallest signs that the wheels are decelerating at the ideal rate: as if in slow motion, they rotate gently just short of locking up, in total contrast to the car, which continues at high speed. At that moment, you realise that the limit of adhesion has been reached and that the braking was impeccable.

Saloon cars equipped with ABS (anti-lock brakes) can achieve this effortlessly. But in competition the parameters of weight, speed and grip are very different and a good driver will achieve a better braking performance than his rivals – particularly on a dry circuit.

■ Braking and changing down

Braking and changing down are two entirely complementary actions. The essentials:

– firstly to brake to the correct entry speed before turning into a corner;
– secondly to change down so that you are in the correct gear at the moment you need to accelerate again.

Downchanging should be completed before you turn into the bend, and thus should be done as you brake, the only available time. It wouldn't do to change down earlier, with the car at full throttle; and to do it later leads to braking, declutching and changing gear in mid-corner, which isn't really desirable.

It should be added that the driver is also helped by simultaneous engine braking when changing down, although that is superfluous in many modern racing cars, which are equipped with mechanical braking to all four wheels.

The rear wheel continues to revolve but the front wheel has nearly – but not totally – locked. Textbook braking...

1

2

4

5

The necessity to brake and change down at the same time leads to another key technique: double-declutching. The 'real' declutch indicates a completed manoeuvre; the 'dummy' is something of a short cut. Double-declutching is imperative for two reasons:

– mechanically, because it is less wearing on the transmission and gearbox;
– dynamically, because it avoids locking wheels and the loss of grip that can entail, with the result that the car's overall balance is better maintained.

You should note that the right foot

3

6

Double-declutching. Along the straight, the accelerator is hard to the floor and the left foot is inactive on its aluminium rest (1). As the corner approaches, the right foot comes off the accelerator and begins to apply the brakes (2). Only now does the left foot come into action as the driver declutches, selects neutral and releases the clutch pedal once more (3). The right foot continues to brake, but the side of the same foot 'blips' the throttle to bring the engine up to optimum revs (4). The left foot again declutches, the required gear is selected, the left foot comes back off the clutch (5) and returns to its rest position. Once the double-declutching operation has been completed, the right foot continues to adjust the braking effort to obtain the ideal entry speed into the corner (6).

A simpler, pseudo form of double-declutching dispenses with the second declutching manoeuvre with the left foot. The 'blip' on the accelerator is given once the left foot on the clutch pedal has disengaged the clutch for the first time. Otherwise, the role of the right foot doesn't change.

cannot, while braking, be released from the pedal in order to actuate the accelerator for either part of the double-declutch procedure. It has therefore to do it at the same time, at the right moment, and in one movement. This action, known as 'heel and toe', is obviously aimed at saving time.

WEIGHT TRANSFER UNDER ACCELERATION

The instant a car accelerates, a proportion of its mass is transferred from the front to the rear wheels. The phenomenon has no effect on steering, but grip at the rear is increased. This explains the superiority of rear-wheel-drive cars when it comes to transmitting high power outputs to the road. Conversely, a front-wheel-drive car is penalised under acceleration. The load on its driven wheels is reduced and torque is less efficiently transmitted to the ground.

The rear-wheel-drive car, on the other hand, benefits from a sort of spiral effect. The harder a driver accelerates, the more weight is transferred to the rear wheels and the more power is efficiently transmitted to the road. There is, of course, a limit...

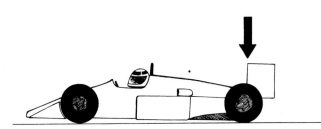

WEIGHT TRANSFER UNDER BRAKING

Under braking, weight is transferred to the front wheels. It is now their turn to benefit from superior grip.

This explains why, in the interests of brake balance, the majority of a car's braking capacity is at the front. That's also why it is often the front wheels which lock first under heavy braking.

If the distribution of the braking effort were identical front and rear, the front wheels would never be sufficiently braked, while the rear wheels, with less load, would be permanently locked.

Weight transfer

At rest, a car has a total given weight, which is divided over the front and rear wheels. On the move, it is continuously subjected to different forces which affect this balance. Thus, for a car weighing 1000 kg at rest, 400

This picture of René Arnoux braking during a right-hander at the French GP in 1988 helps illustrate the phenomenon of weight transfer. The car is well into the corner and the front-right wheel – with less load applied than the front-left – has a natural tendency to lock prematurely. A well-balanced chassis and perfect front/rear brake balance are essential for braking while cornering in this way.

carried by the front wheels and 600 by the rear, the first effect of sharp acceleration will be to lighten the load at the front, which in turn transfers the balance of weight to the rear. It is possible to measure this weight transfer technically, and record variations in terms of tens of kilos.

Under braking, the effect is reversed, weight being transferred from the back to the front. The front wheels could thus 'weigh' 450 kg rather than the normal 400.

When cornering, it is the balance from right to left which is affected: in a right-hand bend, there is more weight on the left. These are all vital differences which must be taken into account when it comes to setting up the chassis. When braking into a corner, the offside of the car will be subject to greater loads and thus have more grip. That's why getting back onto the brakes requires finesse, as it is easier to lock the inside wheels (front and/or rear) than it would be if you braked on the straight, just before the bend.

This weight transfer during braking is the reason for the frontal bias when it comes to brake balance. Thanks to a manual cockpit-adjustment facility, a driver can switch brake bias from front to rear as required. He could, ultimately, shift it all to the front and effectively cut out the rear brakes! Generally, the balance is never set 50/50, as in that circumstance the rear wheels would be prone to early lock-up.

The need to adjust the brake balance varies according to the different levels of grip on the circuit. The less grip there is, the less adhesion the front tyres have and weight transfer is less crucial. To stop this vicious circle, you reduce the effectiveness of the front brakes, to prevent their locking, and increase that of those at the rear. This is the type of adjustment that should be made immediately when there is a significant change in the conditions, notably when it starts to rain.

HOW BEST TO USE YOUR ENGINE

■ The basic goods

To start with, it is either the manufacturer (production engines), the preparation expert (tuned engines) or the design engineer (special racing engines) who provides the three main ingredients for an engine used in competition. That is maximum torque (perhaps at 8500 rpm), maximum power (10,500 rpm) and maximum revs (11,000 rpm).

There is a fourth category, namely the flexibility and power band of an engine. This aspect, although important, can't be measured in numbers, and depends very much upon the driver, who adds the extra elements of driving style and experience to the equation.

It is easy to confuse an engine's torque with its flexibility. The former can be calculated exactly,

while it might be said of an engine that it has greater flexibility because it has a wide power band. In fact, an engine can have low maximum torque yet a wide power band just as easily as it can have high

Ignition is switched on, fuel pumps are primed and the sign of the hand tells the mechanic that all's OK. The silence is about to be broken.

Ayrton Senna limps home with a blown engine. At the peak of the turbo era, engines on maximum boost were putting out nearly 1200 bhp for a modest engine capacity of 1500 cc! Hardly surprising, then, that they were somewhat fragile...

maximum torque and a narrow power band. We find the best examples of such differences between naturally aspirated engines – moderate torque but good flexibility – and forced induction engines – strong torque but generally poor flexibility.

It is equally common to mix up maximum power and maximum revs. The first corresponds with the exact point at which an engine delivers all its available power, while the second depends upon its durability, because beyond that point it could blow up at any second.

It is possible for maximum power and maximum revs to coincide, but by and large an engine will be sound enough mechanically to continue revving after the power curve has started to drop away. Ideally, a good driver strives to maintain engine speed between the point of maximum torque and that of maximum power, because it is between these two extremes that it will operate most effectively.

■ Mistakes to avoid

Over-revving is the most familiar means of a driver harming his engine. There are several ways of doing it, some of which are more damaging than others. Firstly, down a straight, a driver shifting up through the gears may – intentionally or otherwise – go beyond the authorised rev limit. Nowadays, however, only the least sophisticated engines are without electronic rev-limiters, which cut the ignition at a precise, predetermined moment. It has thus become almost impossible to over-rev the engine in this way.

Moving on, the braking area provides a second opportunity for over-revving, as the driver brakes and changes down simultaneously. This can have more serious consequences for the engine, as the rev-limiter is unable to intervene. Over-revving is caused here by premature engagement of a lower gear, when the driver fails to slow the car sufficiently yet hurriedly shifts down a gear all the same.

To avoid this sort of mistake, make sure that you are at least a third of the way into the braking zone before you even think about changing down. Then, while maintaining the same intense braking pressure, you should move progressively down through the box until you are in the right gear for that particular corner.

Generally, novices are more concerned with downchanging (double-declutching and heel and toe) than with efficient braking: thus they get the first part right, make a hash of the second and ... the tachometer needle flies past the red warning line! In their defence, it is a difficult thing to get right as there are no clear-cut guidelines about the exact moment at which a lower gear should be engaged. Braking on the limit is a critical aspect of the sport, and doesn't allow the eyes to wander from the road to crib information from the rev-counter. Knowing exactly the right moment at which to change quickly down through the gears, without causing mechanical mayhem, will come naturally to a good driver. In longer braking areas, however, you can use

Alain Prost: 'After every practice session, I go over a map of the circuit with the technicians, indicating which gear I use for each corner. Thanks to data recorded while I'm on the track, they in turn supply me with details of minimum and maximum engine speeds used during the session. Not only does this help me select ideal gear ratios, it also allows me to exploit the engine's potential to the full. As a result, I know precisely where I stand with fuel consumption and how hard I'm pushing the engine during a race.'

certain landmarks (100-yard marker boards, painted lines, bumps in the track) to facilitate judgement of gearchange points.

The third main cause of over-revving is similar in some respects to the first: it occurs coming out of bends, when a driver's attention is so absorbed by controlling his car that he simply forgets to change gear. In such a case, the rev-limiter is of course totally effective.

The risk of over-revving has traditionally been a problem for racing drivers. And the further they progress in the sport, the more highly tuned the engines become and the greater the threat of a breakage, to the point at which an F1 engine might be just 200 revs away from spinning its last.... In order to limit this phenomenon, or rather to stop its spreading, a surveillance system known as the 'black box' has been under development for a long time by critical race technicians – or possibly by Machiavellian team managers! The 'black box' records precisely a driver's every indiscretion. On a traditional rev-counter, such misdemeanours are given away by a second, 'tell-tale' needle, hidden behind the first. This goes round the dial, but doesn't return, and thus records the maximum

Despite the onslaught of computers, telemetry and other high-tech goodies used by increasingly specialised technicians, the quality of the fuel mix – which confirms, or otherwise, the ideal functioning of an engine – is ascertained in the same old way ... by close scrutiny of the spark plugs!

number of revs the driver used when least sympathetic. But so far have electronic advances allowed the 'black box' system to develop that engineers can now tell not only how many times a driver overstepped the mark, but also at exactly which point he did so...

■ The importance of the gearbox

Discuss racing, and you'll inevitably discuss gearboxes with interchangeable ratios. We'll see later on what you need to know in order to match gearing to the peculiarities of individual circuits. However, at some corners it might be that the selected ratios force drivers to choose between two gears. In that case, you look for the advantages and disadvantages of each, and select a compromise. Let's consider the case of a bend which could be taken in either second or third. The first option gives better stability at the end of the deceleration area, thanks to better engine braking, and allows a quicker rate of acceleration. On the other hand, the driver will have to declutch at maximum power on the exit of the bend in order to take third. This is feasible, but not recommended

as it diminishes the grip of the driven wheels at a time when the driver only has his left hand on the steering wheel.

The second option means that you will be down on revs at the end of the braking area, and the lack of effective engine braking can make the car unstable at the turn-in point; then, as you reaccelerate, you will lose a little extra time.

But that is usually compensated for by the fact that you don't need to change gear at the exit of the bend, leaving you unflustered and thus a touch faster. To resolve this type of problem, there are a couple of things you can do, such as to make a note of comparative lap times, or check how many revs you are pulling 200 yards after the bend, before you change up to fourth.

Whatever, you should not use second if that results in over-revving in the middle of the corner, nor rest in third if the motor drops right out of the power band altogether.

Beyond setting up the gear ratios, there is another important aspect of the gearbox: the speed at which a driver gearshifts. This might seem obvious at first, but in reality novices often underestimate the rapidity of movement of experienced drivers.

Each gearchange corresponds to a brief moment in neutral during which the car is no longer driven, and the longer the shift takes the more perceptible this 'stab on the brakes' becomes. Thus taking an identical time shifting the lever from second to third would not have the same consequences as it would from fourth to fifth. Moreover two-tenths of a second lost with each gearchange means a whole second wasted with a six-speed box! With a real racing car, the speed of the gearchange has more to do with the dexterity of the pilot than with any mechanical components.

As so often in motor sport, you will be penalised instantly for any mistake: there is another way of over-revving your engine. The driver declutches and replants his foot hard on the accelerator when he has missed a gear and the car is actually in neutral. More seriously still, he might select a lower gear when he is after the opposite, such as shifting from fourth to third instead of fourth to fifth. At that moment, the risk of damage is considerable as, in addition to what the engine is going through, there is the possibility of locking the driving wheels and losing control.

Once again, there is no obvious solution to this other than the driver's continual awareness ... knowing he's made a mistake before the effects are felt. A good driver would realise that what he had just done didn't feel right without as much as a glance at his right hand. He would respond immediately, repositioning the gear lever correctly and declutching out of suspicion.

A good driver should be able to count a whole season's worth of missed gearshifts on the fingers of one hand.

By winning the 1989 Brazilian Grand Prix, Nigel Mansell and Ferrari took Formula 1 racing into a new era. An electro-magnetic clutch on his car meant that the British driver used his conventional pedal-operated clutch for starting only. Once under way, he was able to move up or down the box with a simple flick of his index fingers on buttons mounted each side of the steering wheel; the right finger to change up, the left finger to change down. The two principal benefits of the system are that gearchanges are much swifter, and that the driver can simultaneously brake and change down for a corner without taking his hands off the wheel. Furthermore, it puts an end to all that toing and froing of the right foot, as the left is free to concentrate on the job of braking.

THE PERFECT LINE

■ Some general points

The racing line serves to reduce the difficulty presented by a corner or a series of bends. It allows a racing car to proceed at the highest possible speed by reducing the natural outline of the corner to its minimum possible angle. For a series of gentle left-right sweeps, you can imagine an almost straight line down which a car can track without any fear of leaving the circuit. This constitutes the image of the perfect racing line (see diagram).

Generally speaking, each racing line is characterised by three points:

– the turn-in point, usually at the end of the braking area, is the moment at which the car enters the corner;
– the clipping point, also known as the apex, is where the car is closest to the inside of the bend; between these first two points lies the slowest part of the corner;
– the exit is the point at which the car straightens up once again, and if all has been done properly will be the fastest part of the corner.

There are a whole multitude of different racing lines, which depend on the characteristics of different corners, but in some circumstances it might also be necessary to find two different lines for the same bend. In looking for the perfect line, you also have to take into account a few points about the driver (his style, whether he is running alone or battling with other cars), the car (type of transmission, overall balance, available power), and of course the corner itself (if it is preceded or followed by an important straight, the quality of the track surface, whether the track is wet or damp). We'll see later, after further chapters and diagrams, all the factors which can influence the study of the best racing line.

These drivers lined up for the Loews hairpin at Monaco graphically illustrate 'the ideal line' between the left-hander at the top of the picture and the hairpin-left just out of shot. The slight right in between is totally eliminated.

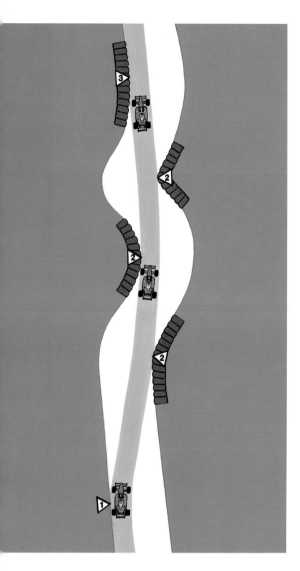

FAST CORNER

Rare indeed are the motor racing circuits which don't include at least one corner of this sort. In this example, the driver turns in (1), passes the apex (2) and conserves his line all the way through the corner (3). The whole operation should be as smooth as possible with no abrupt movements of the steering wheel.

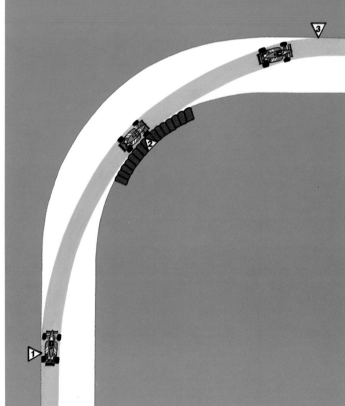

SERIES OF BENDS

This schematic drawing shows how the ideal racing line can all but eliminate some bends. The challenge of this series of bends can in fact be tackled with a minimum of steering effort.

The driver turns in slightly as he approaches the first right-hander (1) to get himself ideally set up at the start. Thereafter, he barely needs to modify his line until the obstacle has been passed.

TIGHT HAIRPIN

The driver purposely turns in late (1), continuing to the outside of the bend in order to create the widest possible angle. In this way, he can treat the remainder of the operation as he would a fast corner. Indeed, his intention must be to be as quick as possible out of the hairpin. To a certain extent, in order to achieve that, he mustn't hesitate to 'sacrifice' the entry phase by turning in somewhat sharply. As soon as the apex has been passed (2), the driver, who has in fact transformed the exit phase into a fast corner, can already begin to accelerate.

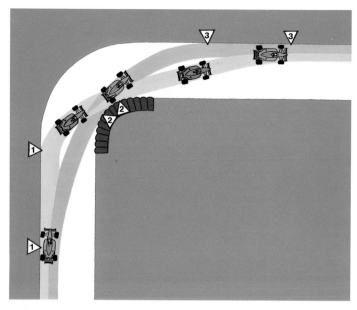

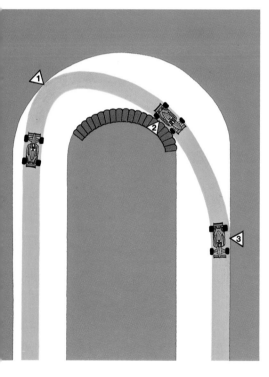

RIGHT-ANGLE TURN

There are countless subtle variations of the textbook technique and all involve turning into corners earlier than normal. They can apply as much to tight hairpins as to fast corners.

Here, the textbook line is illustrated by the red car. Its driver turns in (1) and passes the apex (2) relatively late in order to have a nice clear exit line and be able to accelerate as soon as he's at the apex.

The driver of the green car turns in much earlier and hits the apex sooner than the red car, but he is unable to accelerate out of the corner as early as his rival.

The intention of the first driver is to exit the corner as fast as possible having entered it more slowly. The opposite is true in the second case.

The green car is smoother into the corner and, since braking can be left later, it is a method which obviously favours overtaking into corners.

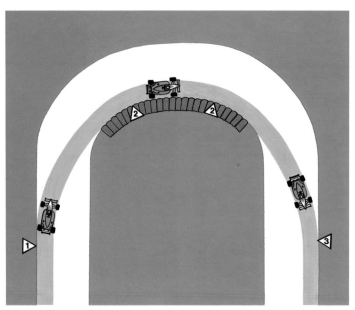

THE LONG CONSTANT-RADIUS CORNER

This type of corner could in fact be described as a very long hairpin. Nevertheless, the apex is too long for there to be any benefit in taking the entry wide as would be the case for a tight hairpin. Here, the driver turns in relatively early and keeps to the inside as long as possible (2). On exit, he is naturally poised to start heading towards the outside (3).

THE OPENING CORNER

The angle of this corner progressively widens. The driver steers in and gets on line early, for he knows that, afterwards, the corner opens out at the very moment he will want to move to the outside. The trick is finding the happy medium between the turning-in and exit points in relation to the increasing radius of the corner.

The final phase of this corner can be treated like a straight and the driver can begin to accelerate.

DOUBLE APEX

It is sometimes possible to find a line which allows a driver to make one corner out of two.

The exit line of the first becomes the entry line for the second, the driver refraining from going too wide so as not to over-tighten the overall corner. The car finds this perfect curve by staying within the inner two-thirds of the track's width. After the first apex, the car is set up for the second without the driver having to make any steering corrections.

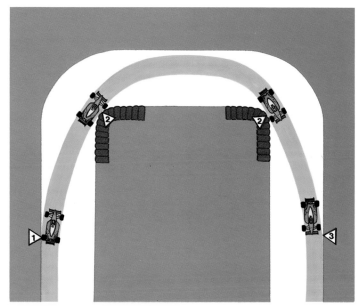

THE TIGHTENING CORNER

The driver stays wide as long as possible in order to hit the apex very late. He brakes and changes down to the selected gear on the outside as he follows the curve of the bend to find the smoothest exit angle possible.

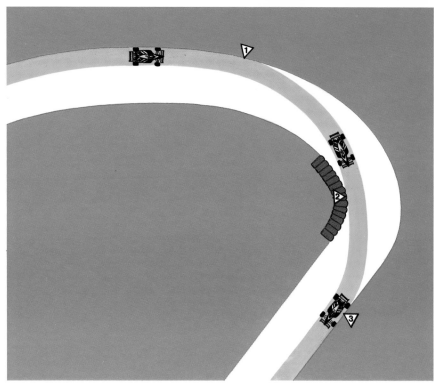

■ One corner on its own

Even though it might nearly involve going off the track, top drivers will always look for the smoothest line possible!

To operate at maximum efficiency, a driver should try and use all the space that's available

to him: the full width of the road, that goes without saying, but also the tiny area separating the track from the run-off area, normally an undulating surface – known as a rumble strip – which is there to dissuade the driver from

wandering any further. So you have to make the circuit as wide as possible, and sometimes a little wider, without damaging the car in any way.

Take a right-hand bend: the driver arrives on the left-hand side of the road, brakes and changes down until coming to the landmark he regards as his turn-in point. Then he turns the car towards the clipping point on the inside of the circuit and, having reached it, he drifts back to the outside towards the exit. Throughout this operation, the driver always tries to get back on the power as early as possible in order to obtain maximum speed at the exit of the corner. We're touching here on a critical point: the best lap time doesn't depend on speed through corners alone; you should never forget the time that can be lost or found on the straight. But the maximum speed you will attain on a straight depends on your exit speed from the previous bend. This can be explained simply in figures.

Exiting a corner at 125 mph rather than 120 mph gives you a 5 mph advantage down the following straight. Supposing that the speed remains constant, after half a mile the difference will be 0.6 second, or around 35 yards.

■ A series of bends

In the case of a series of bends, the driver may not be able to take each in the most efficient manner possible, as it will be the last of them which influences his line. Of course it would be ideal to take them all as quickly as possible, but over a series of three bends the driver should not be afraid of compromising the first two in order to perfect the third, and thus rocket onto the following straight at the highest possible speed (see diagram).

In such a sequence of corners, it is the last which dictates the line through all of them. On the other hand, for a series of bends at the end of a long straight, it isn't unusual to see drivers brake as late as possible to profit from their high speed. They are thus forced to decelerate in the first part of the next bend, known as turning in on the brakes. The longer the straight preceding the corner, the more valuable this technique becomes.

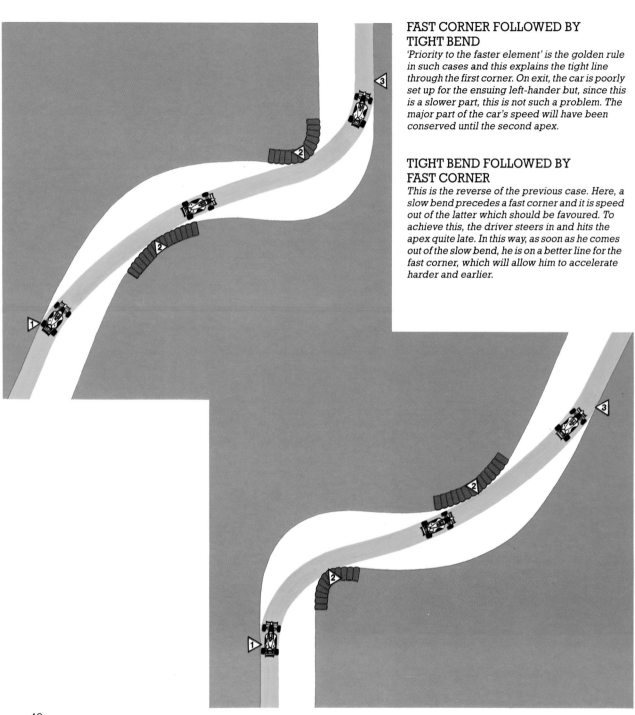

FAST CORNER FOLLOWED BY TIGHT BEND

'Priority to the faster element' is the golden rule in such cases and this explains the tight line through the first corner. On exit, the car is poorly set up for the ensuing left-hander but, since this is a slower part, this is not such a problem. The major part of the car's speed will have been conserved until the second apex.

TIGHT BEND FOLLOWED BY FAST CORNER

This is the reverse of the previous case. Here, a slow bend precedes a fast corner and it is speed out of the latter which should be favoured. To achieve this, the driver steers in and hits the apex quite late. In this way, as soon as he comes out of the slow bend, he is on a better line for the fast corner, which will allow him to accelerate harder and earlier.

TWO IDENTICAL BENDS FOLLOWED BY A STRAIGHT

Here, it is important to note that it isn't the type of bend which determines the racing line (the two bends being of equal difficulty) but the fact that it is either preceded or followed by a long straight.

The driver steers in very late, sacrificing the first part of the right-hander to hit the apex well inside. In this way, he is set to take the following left-hander as though he hadn't been at all handicapped by the preceding right.

The first corner is sacrificed for optimal exit speed, which will benefit the car all along the ensuing straight.

TWO IDENTICAL BENDS PRECEDED BY A STRAIGHT

Unlike the above drawing, the driver here is finishing a long straight. In order to conserve built-up speed as long as possible, he lengthens the straight by steering in early in order to brake as late as possible. The first corner is taken as though the second didn't exist, even if the driver then finds himself on a less good line for the second. The loss is not too serious since the second bend was slow. Speed is not required for an ensuing straight so, overall, less time is lost this way.

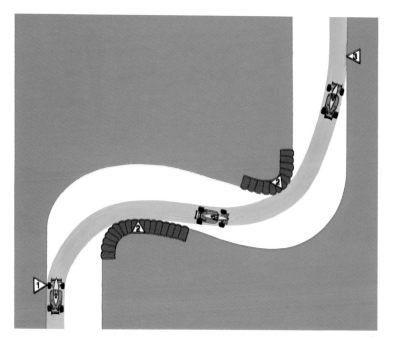

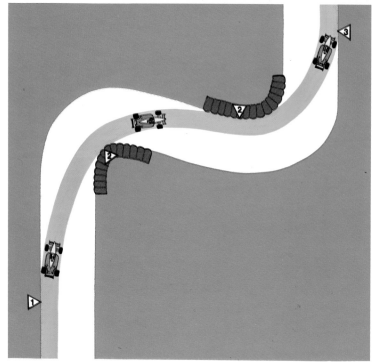

CONTROLLING A CAR AT THE LIMIT

■ The three types of transmission

There are three different groups of car, each identified by its transmission, each of which consequently demands a different technique.

Rear-wheel drive

On this type of car, the front wheels' sole purpose is to steer, and the rears transmit the power. This is the most efficient set-up for speed events on a circuit.

When weight transfers to the rear of the car, it benefits by making maximum use of all its available torque. In circuit terms, this form of transmission is the easiest to handle and the most effective.

Front-wheel drive

In this instance, both power and steering are directed through the front wheels, the rears remaining free.

Following the principle of weight transfer once more, the lightening of the front wheels under acceleration considerably reduces their effectiveness and thus limits the usable power. Consequently, this type of transmission is generally less effective on racing circuits, a few rare exceptions notwithstanding, but has its advantages in road events where maximum power is not called into play so often.

Four-wheel drive

This system has only been used in motor sport for a few seasons. Power is split to all four wheels, and torque distribution may vary from front to rear. The front wheels naturally do the steering. Under acceleration, weight transfer no longer reduces the grip of the front wheels, and thus the level of overall traction is vastly superior to that of other types of transmission. Four-wheel drive has thus found a niche in all forms of motor sport where natural grip is limited, such as rallies and rally-raids.

Although there have been recent cases of success for four-wheel-drive cars on racing circuits, the latter's characteristics don't generally favour this type of transmission. Firstly there is a significant weight handicap (due to the two drivetrains), which often cannot be overcome. Thanks to the high speeds achieved by single-seaters and sports-prototypes, designers have been able to achieve a superior level of grip with a smaller weight penalty by using various aerodynamic devices.

■ Controlling rear-wheel drive

Among true circuit racers, whether single-seaters or sports-prototypes, there are no front- or four-wheel-drive applications, only rear-wheel drive. The basis for the perfect control of a single-seater or a sports-prototype thus comes from the steering wheel and throttle pedal in equal measure. The latter controls the rear wheels under acceleration or deceleration while the steering wheel maintains overall balance by means of the front wheels.

What is evident in racing may not be so for your everyday car. This is simply due to its relative lack of power in relation to its total weight.

For a 600 kg racing car with 500 bhp, the response of the rear wheels to the accelerator is immediate. It bears no relation to that in a car weighing twice as much endowed with a third of the power.

Good control and perfect balance are obtained through the use of both hands (on the steering wheel) and the right foot (on the throttle).

Before going into the various means of controlling a car, it is best to split corners into two categories, based upon the speed at which they can be negotiated.

A slow corner is one taken at below 60–75 mph; any faster, and it becomes a quick corner. That can't be taken as a complete generalisation, however, for much depends on the configuration of the circuit, the potential of the car and, naturally, the skill and experience of the driver.

Slow corners

For this type of bend, it is best to have an oversteering car, that is one which slides more at the rear than it does at the front. It is thus an agile car, pivoting around itself, and it is also efficient. By turning more than the radius of the bend, it reaches the exit more quickly, which constitutes time saved.

The slower the corner, the more you need to 'place' the car neatly. Turning the wheel onto the correct line you must be quick and incisive without exaggerated movement; turn it too much and you will achieve the opposite

effect to that desired.

Then, the driver must wait before accelerating so that the rear wheels don't bite too early. You enter this type of corner under full deceleration, the rear wheels slowed only by engine braking. That is the point at which they have their least grip, which makes the car all the more lively at the entry to the corner. Then it will oversteer increasingly until the driver feels it is time to retake control. At first you do this via the throttle:

– if you apply a lot of power in a long corner, you can hold the slide for a reasonable distance;
– if you apply limited power, or it is a short corner, you can balance and stop the slide by thus restoring grip to the rear wheels.

At the same time, you bring the front wheels back into play. If that isn't enough, you apply opposite lock – that's to say steer in the opposite direction to the corner – to restore balance and regain control. Opposite lock demands extremely quick and exact movements.

It can happen that you overdo the steering input at such a time, or that, having done it, you wait too long before straightening out the front wheels. This is a common mistake made by beginners – or experienced, but unskilled, drivers – and it results in the car shooting back to the other side of the circuit, oversteering in the opposite direction. This is often sharper and more deceptive than the original oversteer; it is thus much more difficult to master as the front wheels are all of a sudden on full opposite lock in the wrong direction! It is thus imperative to straighten the front wheels just as soon as you have corrected the oversteer. It should be stressed that strong oversteer may require double the steering corrections, and that perfect control will only be retained once the car has returned to complete stability down the following straight.

Fast corners

Bearing in mind what has just been written, the complete opposite applies here. It is essential that the car does not oversteer, for two reasons:

– it is very difficult to catch the slide;
– you scrub off too much speed, which costs time.

Oversteer, a useful asset in slow corners, is costly in faster curves. Having reached its limit of

UNDERSTEER

The rear wheels of the car adhere perfectly, but the front wheels have lost grip and can no longer react to the driver's steering instructions.

The rear wheels continue to power the car, which will start to drift to the outside if the driver doesn't take preventative action. This he can do in two ways: lifting off the accelerator will cause the rear wheels to 'push' less and allow the front to regain grip progressively. If that isn't sufficient, braking during the turn (taking care not to lock the wheels, of course) will slow the car and allow the front to grip once more.

NEUTRAL HANDLING

The lateral drift of the rear wheels is equal to that of the front. All four wheels slide in the same way. The front wheels are straight and the driver doesn't need to steer, since the car was set up on entry into the corner.

This is the ideal compromise. Control of power to the rear wheels, by means of the accelerator, and control of the front, by means of steering instructions, becomes a somewhat easier matter since the corrections required are less important.

Despite what the drawing might suggest, the car isn't about to mount the outside kerb since forward movement cancels out lateral momentum.

OVERSTEER

There is no problem with grip at the front here, but traction at the rear has been lost. This might be a result of the car's overall balance which has been purposely set up in this way, or it might be a result of too much power. In the latter case it is the spinning rear wheels which cause the rear end to slide out. That might result in the car pivoting on itself and eventually spinning.

The driver has two options to regain control:
– firstly, opposite lock might be sufficient to re-establish the car's balance;
– if that doesn't suffice, lifting off the accelerator will result in a drop of speed and will help give traction to the rear wheels once more, especially if the original reason for the oversteer was too much power.

In some situations, an experienced driver might not in fact lift off but rather accelerate slightly to provide traction at the rear again.

adhesion, it is better for a car to understeer lightly in such circumstances.

A gentle touch is required on the steering wheel as you turn in, the more so the faster you are travelling. Nobody should get the idea that a violent twitch of the wheel is required when entering a corner above 75 mph! The driver should follow the racing line and power through progressively; right through the bend, he should try and draw a perfect curve. In the interests of keeping the car balanced, you should not enter the corner with the rear wheels decelerating: the oversteer you look for in slower corners is amplified here by the greater speed, and the car will snap sideways. From the moment he commits the car, the driver should have his foot on the throttle: that doesn't mean you have to have it hard down, simply that you should avoid entering a fast corner under deceleration.

After braking and changing down on the previous straight, you should reapply the throttle in the few yards before the entry to the corner, i.e. just before the turn-in point. The rear wheels regain their traction and the whole drivetrain is restored to full grip. The car is 'sucked' to the ground, and the first things to reach their limit of adhesion will be the front wheels. The resulting gentle understeer gives the car stability through fast corners and, as the front wheels have only a mild angle of drift, hardly any time is lost. If there is too much understeer, it can be resolved via the throttle pedal: a slight lift will produce a small reduction in the amount of understeer; a sudden, sharp lift will momentarily reduce the grip of the rear wheels in favour of the fronts. Backing off for a long period may provoke instability, and a car that was understeering a few moments ago may suddenly snap into oversteer.

All these corrections should be carried out smartly – no more than an inch or two of movement from the right foot – something which will only come with experience.

In summary, oversteer in a sharp bend can be controlled by swift application of corrective lock, while fast-corner understeer can be adjusted by the opening or closing of the throttle.

■ Controlling front-wheel drive

The main difference is the reduced role of the throttle pedal, which is used here in conjunction with steering inputs.

Slow corners

In spite of everything, there are a few things in common with rear-wheel drive:

– use of the steering wheel must always be incisive and swift;
– you leave the throttle relaxed to enable the front end to turn into the corner better and allow the rear to oversteer.

Reapplying pressure to the accelerator does not control the rear of the car in the manner we saw previously; on the contrary, in this case it affects the front wheels. Hence the necessity to position a front-wheel-drive car more accurately than you would its RWD equivalent. Moreover the driven front wheels help the car to correct itself and reduce the need for opposite lock.

As the car reacts so differently to RWD, you have to act accordingly: reaccelerate sharply (with no fear of a spin) but with less opposite lock. Failing which, you will over-correct the front wheels and the car will at worst spear off the track on the outside, at best zig-zag down the centre of the circuit, at the risk of sudden loss of control.

Front-wheel-drive cars have a tendency not to want to turn into corners. It is known that they are not completely at home on the race track, but that they are much better suited to rallying, or indeed any form of competition where there is less grip. In such difficult conditions, the driver can employ two subtle techniques to increase the efficiency of front-wheel drive while negating its chronic tendency to understeer.

The 'pendulum'

This driving technique, pioneered by Scandinavian rally drivers, amounts to steering the wrong way before entry to a bend. So, approaching a right-hander, you don't approach on the left-hand side of the road, as you might imagine, but on the right. At the last possible moment, the driver flicks to the left, then swerves sharply right, making full use of the pendulum effect to commit the front wheels to the desired line. Sometimes, even this may not be enough, in which case three movements may be required: start with the car on the left, steer once to the right, then once to the left, then flick to the right again to tackle the corner.

You won't find this technique used at all on circuits, but only in rallies, where gravel, snow and other surface conditions offer so little grip.

Left-foot braking

This is another technique originally developed by the Scandinavians, who are renowned as experts at driving on snow. It has since been widely copied: it involves braking with the left foot all the way through a corner, while the right continues to accelerate.

The approach to the corner – braking and downchanging – takes place as normal. But from the turn-in point, before the apex, the right foot is on the throttle, the left on the brake.

It is a simple phenomenon to understand. The accelerator lessens the effect of the brake on the front wheels, through which the power is transmitted. The rears, on the other hand, lock up. The resultant loss of grip makes it easier for the driver to pitch the car into oversteer. Throughout the corner, the continual acceleration and braking unsettles the car and allows the driver to avoid any understeer. This technique, like the 'pendulum', is more commonly used when grip is at a minimum.

On the other hand, it is less advisable on a good, dry road, where there is plenty of grip and it is harder for a driver to unsettle the car. You should also note that it is hard on machinery. It destroys the front brakes, as the wheels are subjected to simultaneous accelerative and decelerative forces; the rear is not affected.

Specialists of this discipline often talk about it as though it were quite normal. In reality, there are few drivers who can use it to good effect. In order to profit from it, you need talent, experience and lots of practice. It was always a joke among older drivers to say: 'If you have a young rival who's bothering you by going too fast, tell him all about the benefits of left-foot braking and front-wheel drive. You'll be left in peace for the rest of the season. It shouldn't take him more than a year to master the technique!'

Normally, braking bias on rally cars is to the rear. This imbalance is intentional. It allows the driver to avoid locking the front wheels and subsequent understeer, at the cost of locking the rears, which facilitates entry to corners.

Fast corners

A front-wheel-drive car behaves

like a RWD car in quick corners: the driver is already on the throttle before he turns in, and you should try to avoid roughness at the wheel, always looking for the smoothest line possible. In these circumstances, control is easier than it is with a RWD car, as movements on the throttle pedal don't affect the rear of the car. However, you can always counteract excessive understeer through adjustment of the accelerator; and you can fully open the throttle appreciably earlier than you might in a rear-wheel-drive car.

In conclusion, a front-drive car, out of sorts in a tight corner, is most effective in quick corners thanks to its natural affinity for understeer.

■ Controlling four-wheel drive

Like front-wheel drive, 4WD only features rarely at the highest echelons of circuit racing, and for the moment there are no single-seaters nor any sports-prototypes featuring this kind of transmission. In contrast, it is widely used in rallies on account of its marvellous traction. The lack of grip has always been a key problem in events taking place on public roads, and in order to make the best use of all available power good traction is invaluable. This explains the domination of four-wheel-drive cars in top-level rallying since 1981.

Basically, a four-wheel-drive car is similar to a FWD car in its behaviour. You can treat it as two-thirds front-wheel drive, one-third RWD. Everything depends on the torque split, decided by the engineers, who are able to adjust it according to the different types of terrain on which the car has been developed.

There is never a systematic 50/50 split. When grip is minimal, it may come close to that. But if there is more grip, as on tarmac on a sunny day, the temptation is to decrease the power of the front wheels in favour of the rears, in order to reproduce the natural balance of a RWD car.

The effect on cars with variable torque split can be seen in the way they are driven. If the driver chooses a 50/50 balance, he has a car with FWD characteristics; if he prefers just 25 per cent of the power at the front, 75 at the rear, the handling will be closer to that of a RWD car.

The four-wheel-drive Renault 21 Turbo took the French production car championship in 1988. This photo shows it in typical 4WD posture coming out of this bend, i.e. neutral to slight understeer, as can be seen by the slight turning in of the front wheels.

Slow corners

In the first part of such corners, a 4WD produces RWD behaviour as the car decelerates. Then, as you accelerate past the apex, the understeer you associate with FWD takes over. As with front-wheel drive, it is best to avoid excessive opposite lock, relying rather on the accelerator to maintain control at the exit.

Fast corners

If a driver arrives in a fast corner and lifts off, he will upset the balance of the car and risk putting it sideways. So again it's best to get back on the throttle before taking the racing line, and only then should you start to move the steering wheel progressively.

Left-foot braking

The 'pendulum' technique, encountered in the section on FWD cars, can gainfully be employed with 4WD machines on slippery surfaces. Left-foot braking is rather less spectacular. Unlike front-wheel drive, the rear wheels are not free when the brakes are applied, and all four wheels are subjected to contradictory forces. And the fiercest stab on the brakes won't be enough to lock the rear wheels alone. In theory, it serves no purpose. In spite of which, several drivers use the technique, which can be explained in several ways:

– firstly drivers have often been schooled in FWD cars, so it is a technique that they have always been used to;
– secondly, in turbocharged cars, this style of driving allows the driver to keep the turbo spinning, and thus the car responds immediately when he releases his left foot;
– the third, and last, is that a car subjected to simultaneous forces of braking and acceleration has a tendency to load up its rear suspension. This alters the balance of the car, often to the driver's liking. At the same time, stamping on the brakes just before the car takes off over a yump can reduce the time it spends in the air.

If drivers who use this technique are few and far between nowadays – and most of them are Scandinavians – it is worth noting that several manufacturers have thought it worthwhile developing an electronic clutch, thus freeing the left foot to concentrate on other things...

DIFFERENT LEVELS
OF GRIP

Grip is a major aspect of race driving. There are hundreds of different levels which the driver must be able to recognise, analyse and handle. The available grip is dependent on two key elements: the type of car you are driving and, especially,

the nature of the road surface.

It is said that a car has good roadholding when it generates high levels of grip. This is down to factors beyond the driver (weight distribution, transmission, type of suspension), or alternatively down to things he may have

WET-WEATHER LINES

The orange line depicts the classic line for this type of corner in dry weather. The blue line shows how the ideal line through the same corner changes in the wet.

Approaching the corner, the yellow car takes up position in the middle of the track, avoiding the outside line where the surface is likely to be worn by the repeated passage of racing cars and soiled by deposits of rubber and oil. In this way, the car benefits from a cleaner, less damaged surface offering superior grip in rain. Then, instead of turning in normally, the driver cuts across the classic line before hugging it on the outside.

Until the corner has been completed and the driver can revert to the normal line, he should always be looking for parts of the track which offer optimum grip.

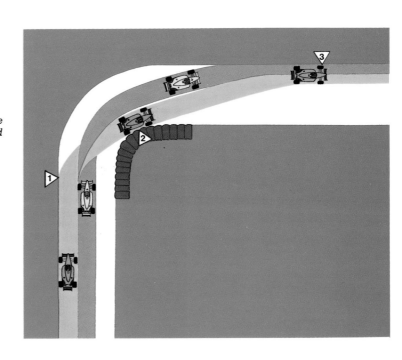

chosen (tyres, suspension settings, aerodynamic balance). But the main concern for drivers is the vast number of different surfaces encountered in motor sport. They can be broken down into two general categories: circuit racing and rallying.

■ Circuit: dry, damp and wet conditions

Tarmac circuits offer the greatest grip when they are little used, clean and dry. Those are typical track conditions. But beyond that, there are numerous factors which can play a part: the quality of the

Alain Prost in torrential rain at Spa during the 1988 Belgian Grand Prix coming out of Raidillon at more than 125 mph. Power to grip ratio in such conditions is not far from that of a rally car ... on ice!

track surface (whether it's bumpy, damaged or worn); the weather (hot, cold, damp or rainy); and the presence of particles of dust, rubber and/or oil.

A good driver will appreciate all these factors, which might change from one circuit to another, or even from one lap to the next. Braking is the first area in which it is important to take stock of the available grip. Whether you over- or underestimate the level of grip in a braking area, you achieve the same effect – loss of time. Overestimation causes you to brake too late, so that you spend the first part of the corner struggling to keep the car on the track, when you should have been back on the power; at worst, it can result in total loss of control. Underestimation means that you brake too early, the only effect of which is that it has on your lap times. Finding the ideal entry speed into a corner is a vital part of the racing driver's job. Adjusting the lateness of his braking a fraction at a time, he will eventually find the best solution and improve his entry speed into the corner by several miles per hour.

There is a fine line between overestimating and underestimating the available level of grip, which makes it all the more difficult to establish.

Unlike events elsewhere, circuit racing demands that the driver should have intimate knowledge of every inch of the track. The tiniest change in the surface, which might affect the available grip, is taken into consideration: fresher tarmac here or there, joins in the track surface, dips or bumps, the gradient and camber of the surface, drops of rain, a low kerb that you should use to your advantage...

From this, a circuit racer can discover the absolute limit, although that requires a certain style of driving. Contrary to what most onlookers might think – or notice – a single-seater or sports-prototype travelling at the limit will be sliding gently but constantly. But the good driver should avoid allowing the car to break away excessively (with either over- or understeer), as that carries severe penalties. In the short term, it ruins lap times; later on, it will cause the tyres to overheat prematurely.

When grip levels are high, the trick is to remain a fraction below the limit, appreciating that the better the grip the greater the speed and precision needed to control a car's reactions.

◼ Rallying: gravel, snow and ice

It's in rallying and its numerous derivatives that you encounter the greatest variety of conditions. These range from tarmac (usually in worse condition than that found on circuits) to snow in all its forms (fresh, packed, thawing), via ice (in patches, or concentrated as on frozen lakes) and gravel (smooth and fast, rough and rocky, sandy and muddy). This fabulous mosaic of radically different surfaces has one common factor: all surfaces encountered in rallying have a lot less grip than their circuit racing equivalents.

The second striking difference between these two forms of competition is that it is totally impossible to know a rally route as well as you might the small, but significant, nuances of a racing circuit. This is a reasonable assumption, for despite the accuracy and the depth of a co-driver's notes, a circuit is usually only two or three miles long, while the rally will take place over several hundred miles. The rally driver thus has to improvise rather more than his circuit counterpart. To employ circuit techniques to try and discover the limit in a rally would be a catastrophic mistake. The tricky surfaces and the less exact nature of the route create an explosive cocktail, which can lead to accidents as cars understeer straight off before they've even been able to start making a turn.

That's why rally drivers seek to keep the rear of their cars on an uneven keel. This position of apparently chronic oversteer allows them either to attack a corner, or to drive defensively: if the corner is faster than anticipated, they reduce the drift of the rear wheels in order to use all the available road; if, on the other hand, they find a corner tighter than expected, they increase the oversteer, which pivots the car further around the bend while at the same time scrubbing off speed.

Thus you can see how the driving styles demanded by the two different disciplines are completely opposite. A rally car would be ineffective, undrivable and indeed dangerous if used on a circuit, while ideal settings for the race track would have similarly perverse effects if deployed in a rally, promoting enormous understeer and a general lack of manageability.

Former World Rally Champion Juha Kankkunen demonstrates four-wheel drift during the 1987 Monte Carlo Rally. The front wheels of his Lancia Delta HF are practically straight and the Finnish driver powers the four-wheel-drive car through with constant control of the accelerator pedal. The Lancia's torque split – slightly in favour of the rear wheels – certainly helps him in his task, but Kankkunen has used all his skill to set the car up in advance for the corner.

ANTICIPATION

In perfect control and sliding at the limit of adhesion, there are things which a driver must feel, and which are difficult to explain. Thus, having turned into a slow corner, yet without accelerating, he knows that his car will slide at the rear. But only his feel for the car will let him know the exact moment and extent of the oversteer.

Expect too much, and you run the risk of letting the car pivot round into a complete spin as the rear is travelling faster than the front. Apply opposite lock or reaccelerate too quickly and you'll counter the oversteer too soon. This isn't serious in as far as you won't lose control, but it's inefficient. The ideal lies somewhere between these two extremes. The earlier you spot the slide, the better you can react, everything being a matter of feeling. People talk of reflexes, but a reflex reaction comes in response to an unexpected situation.

A driver acts upon anticipation rather than reflex. The action should result from the successful co-ordination of quick, precise movements which always precede the car's reactions.

The sequence of actions needed to take a corner is logical and complete, without room for improvisation. Reflexes only come into play when the driver is taken by surprise: the patch of oil on the circuit, the sudden, unforeseen mechanical problem, or any other hazard that wasn't there the previous lap.

■ Reference points

On a track, you first study the lines. To help with that, you look for as many reference points as possible around the circuit.

Naturally, these include the braking distance marker boards before corners. Generally, a driver can rely on boards being placed 300, 200 and 100 yards from the theoretical turn-in point, at the entry to the bend. But you also need more exact, subtle assistance, which may be exclusive to you.

That could be anything from the point at which the track surface alters to a blob of paint, via an advertising hoarding, or indeed a small bump which you feel every lap. These landmarks are as vital on the straight as they are in a corner, braking zone or acceleration area. In this way, the driver gets to learn every yard of the circuit. Hence he knows exactly when to brake before a corner, steer, accelerate and change up on the following straight.

Once these reference points are established, the driver is in a position to think ahead about everything he is doing.

So, when on the straight,

accelerating and changing up through the box, your eye will already be fixed on the reference point you use to denote the start of the braking area. You stick to this as closely as possible. As you brake, your mind should be on

Especially before it was modified, the Hunaudières Straight at Le Mans was a place where drivers, travelling in the region of 225 mph (i.e. around 100 yards per second!), had to show extreme anticipation.

However fast the reactions of the best of them might be, they could never be less than a couple of tenths of a second. In that space of time, if a problem should arise, a car would already have travelled 30 or 40 yards. Even in the best of cases, that is greater than the distance between the guard rails at either side. It is therefore essential that a driver foresees potential problems and anticipates what preventative measures he might need to take.

the turn-in point, at the end of the braking area. The car is turning into the bend, but your mind is already on the apex. There, you are thinking about the exit, where your attention turns to your next landmark, somewhere down the subsequent straight. A good driver thus anticipates constantly. A bad driver is one who seeks, spots and analyses the same series of reference points too late to act upon them. If he discovers trouble the moment his car hits it, everything is proceeding too quickly for him. He is thus incapable of taking on board all this information at once, and must therefore slow down.

The good driver is way ahead of what he is doing. According to a well-known analogy used by Jackie Stewart, he is taking part in a sort of slow-motion film: the slower it seems, the better his anticipation and the faster he goes. That might explain the display of calm at 185 mph.

He is in control of himself every bit as much as he is of the car.

Alternatively, the faster the 'film' rolls, the more events speed up and the slower the driver. That could be down to a lack of fitness, or even a complete lack of ability! From that moment, everything is in a rush: speed exceeds control and the car is not used to its full potential.

■ Feel for the car

It is essential to develop a feeling for the car, and – as described at the start of the chapter – to become as one with it.

The driver should feel his car throughout his body, his back, his kidneys ... everywhere: the moment when the front breaks loose, that when the rear end starts to slide. This vibration indicates a wheel is about to lock up, that light imbalance tells you that the car isn't quite straight under braking...

Without this sensitivity, the car will be well off the racing line before the driver realises it. And if he isn't aware of any problem almost before it arises, any remedial action via the throttle or steering wheel will be too late and ineffective. A driver who is slow to appreciate situations isn't in control of events: he is permanently forced to try and redress mistakes, to the detriment of his lap times. Those who pick up the first hints of trouble are able to react before it happens, which gives them a huge advantage over their less gifted rivals. To be well driven, a car must be felt almost viscerally, as though it were an extension of the driver's limbs.

Even the best of them can lose control at times, including triple World Champion Nelson Piquet, seen here in difficulty during the 1985 Brazilian Grand Prix.

THE 'STRAIGHT ON' OR THE 'EMERGENCY' LINE

Whatever the profile of the corner, a driver might have to resort to this solution if confronted with a serious mechanical problem (unbalanced car, brake problems, etc) or following a major driving error (over-optimistic entry speed into the corner, braking too late, etc).

In such cases, the driver should seek to increase his braking distance by prolonging the preceding straight as much as possible. Braking distance can be as much as doubled in this way.

Clearly, this will cost the driver time, but avoiding going off the track has become the prime consideration to the detriment of optimum efficiency through the corner.

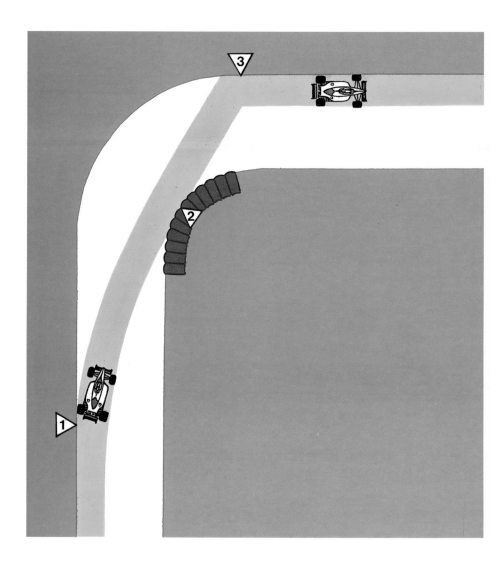

LOSS OF CONTROL BEFORE THE APEX

Generally, when a driver loses control before the apex, the car has a tendency to head towards the outside of the corner.

Unless the incident is the result of a mechanical failure (in which case the car would go straight on without spinning) or the result of a driver error (overestimation of entry speed), the car maintains a certain inertia as it spins and will tend to follow an arc loosely parallel to the corner itself.

As soon as the driver realises that he is about to lose control of his car, he must brake as hard as possible – no half-measures! – until he has stopped. With luck, he might come to a halt on the track, otherwise emergency braking will at least have reduced his speed as he goes off.

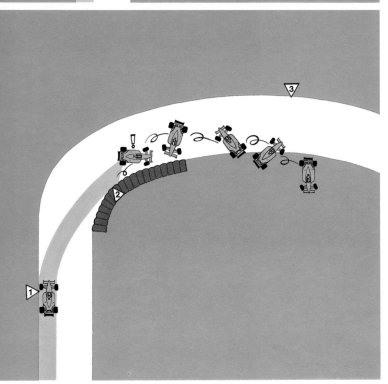

LOSS OF CONTROL AFTER THE APEX

When a driver loses control after the apex, the car is generally under acceleration, giving it added energy as it spins and causing it to turn sharply towards the inside of the track.

Here again, the driver should brake heavily as soon as he realises he has lost control. In this way, he will have a greater chance of remaining on the track, since the car will have a tendency to follow the profile of the corner itself as it spins.

Alain Prost's comments

Installation in the car

Before turning a wheel, there is one thing which is very important and is worthy of mention: the adaptation of the driver to the car. Seat location and driving position aren't talked about very often, because they are usually taken for granted. But for me such things are of fundamental importance. I remember in 1988, with McLaren, I had five or six different seats made before I found one I was happy with. The mechanics had moved around the pedals, steering wheel and gear lever, but I never found a satisfactory driving position! Thus I could probably lap just as fast as usual, but as I wasn't comfortable I had to stop every three laps or so because of cramp. As I said, it is essential that you are perfectly comfortable in a car before you so much as turn a wheel.

And each driver has his own tastes: Niki Lauda and I employed totally different positions: he lay down a little more in his car; in the footwell, I preferred to have the brake pedal a little closer than the accelerator, while Lauda liked them both at the same distance. For my part, I have the steering wheel very close to the instrument panel because I sit quite close up, and I have the gear lever at a slight angle, while Lauda used to have it canted right over. Such preferences don't stop you driving a car if it's any other way, but you wouldn't be able to give it your best.

Sitting on the floor

There are many cars which don't have a rest for the left foot, and that is a big mistake! Of course you can drive without it, and that has happened to me. But to drive really quickly, particularly in fast corners, it's impossible. You lose too much of your feeling for the car.... In any case, if one isn't properly installed, one can't appreciate the reactions of the car or its settings.

For my part, I have another little trick which I have always used, which consists of sitting on the floor of the tub. Many drivers have a foam seat which reaches to the bottom of the car. I think that's stupid. I have much greater sensitivity for the car through sitting directly on the floor. You don't have to be held firmly in an all-enveloping seat. It's important that the shoulders and hips should be held firmly but I don't like to be wholly restrained, apart from by the safety harness.

'It is essential to be perfectly at one with the car in order to sense its slightest reactions.'

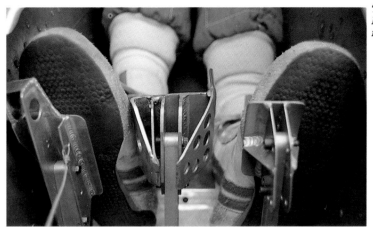

'Even in Formula 1, you can have a pedal-box without a footrest for the left foot!'

Should you double-declutch?

Generally when downchanging I go directly from the gear I'm in at the end of a straight to the one I need for the next corner: from sixth to second, for instance. I bypass all the gears in between. If it's sometimes possible to hear a couple of blips on the throttle, it's only during lengthy braking manoeuvres where for me it's a question of keeping the engine within the power band, rather than having to rev it at the moment where I would otherwise effectively need to double-declutch. I don't see the point in going right down through all the gears, but it's a question of whatever you yourself feel happiest doing, the main thing being to concentrate upon the braking when all's said and done. However, under hard braking or in the wet it's often worthwhile not to jump straight down the box in order to maintain the stability of the rear wheels.

As for double-declutching, it's something I do systematically, even if in a hurry it may seem brief, like a 'false' double-declutch. But I think it's essential you know how to do it. It won't matter over the course of a race; it will be more important over a whole season, and during the length of your career it will be invaluable. It's things like that that make you different from your team-mate and rivals: you miss fewer gears, do less damage to the gearbox, are a better driver for it and enjoy an enhanced reputation...

Racing lines in the wet

There is no firm rule about racing lines in the wet. On fast circuits, it's often advantageous to stick to the outside, running alongside the dry racing line. This is because that part of the track won't be covered in tiny rubber deposits, which are notoriously slippery in the wet.

But on a damp track, each driver has his own ideas about the best lines, and that can go from one extreme to another at the same corner: some stick to the inside, others to the outside, and there's barely any difference at the exit! Sometimes it's quite bizarre. There is, however, one thing that's certain. Be wary of trackside kerbs, which are terribly slippery in the wet, especially those that have been painted.

'The smaller the run-off areas, the higher the price you pay for the slightest error in the rain. So, in Monaco...'

The pros and cons of different styles

For a driver who turns in early, as Jacques Laffite and I do, it's as much a means of defence as attack. It helps you avoid some of the specific problems at the entry to a corner, but if the circuit is greasy at the exit you tend to skate straight off.... Drivers like Keke Rosberg or the late Gilles Villeneuve were always on the ragged edge at the entry to a corner, which meant that a change in the level of grip might take them unpleasantly by surprise on the exit. In reality, they were never taken by surprise, or at least a lot less than we were.... A driver like Rosberg could never adapt to my driving style, whereas from time to time I adopted his. Perhaps not always, but certainly sometimes, and I think that was certainly an advantage for me. From the spectators' point of view, however, an attacking driving style is certainly preferable. It has never been proved that either of these two styles is appreciably faster than the other. I personally think that mine is 'quicker' over the course of a season, in that it limits the possibility of mistakes. I'm convinced of it! Note that cars lend themselves more or less to any style of driving.

  The difference between Keke Rosberg's style and mine would be more striking in the wet.... In difficult conditions of this kind, I always force myself to drive astutely, trying to exploit any available traction to its best effect, and I always look for the smoothest, neatest lines. As for Keke, he'd arrive with all wheels locked up – I'm not exaggerating! – sideways as he turned in, spinning the wheels, leaping over kerbs on the exit and winding up with two wheels on the grass! Certainly spectacular, and at one point during the corner doubtless a couple of tenths quicker than me.... But on the other hand I don't think he'd be faster than me over a whole lap.

Attacking drivers

I did see both Keke Rosberg and Gilles Villeneuve driving almost sedately. But they were capable of doing things that I barely know how to do, or at least only in exceptional circumstances.

It is a brutal form of driving which, in a way, owes nothing to the car, its set-up or its fine tuning.... For my part, I prefer to drive according to the settings I have chosen, then to change them depending upon what I've subsequently noticed. But for some drivers, their settings and the handling of the car were of little consequence: it had to be driven like that simply because they wanted to!

'It's not surprising that a chassis is worn out and ready to be changed after just a few races, even if it hasn't been involved in a shunt!'

'My first and only experience of rallying was the Rallye du Var in southern France in 1982. It is a sport which calls for much more intuition and improvisation than racing.'

Mechanical sympathy

It isn't a myth to say that some drivers abuse their equipment more than others. There are many very good drivers, who have lots of experience and are very good at development work, but are forever breaking cars! It's down to a driving style, a way of ill-treating the car which, while travelling at the same speed as anyone else, provokes a faster rate of wear and tear in every department: tyres, brakes, gearbox, engine, fuel consumption...

In the course of an event, this difference between two drivers is important; over a season, decisive; so throughout a career...

My only experience of rallying

I had only ever raced single-seaters, so it was interesting to discover a different form of motor sport. The first thing I recall is the extraordinary ambience you find in rallying. The hardest thing, in practical terms, was my time spent on reconnaissance, as I had everything to learn. Technically, rally driving appeared to be a totally different art. You always have to leave a margin for error, as it's impossible to take every corner at the limit, as I do – almost to the millimetre – on a circuit. You have to adopt quite a different approach to your driving: more feeling, more improvisation, more perception. As for fine tuning, there are very few things you can change compared with what you can do to a single-seater.

Finally, even if I enjoyed myself enormously, I can't say I felt at ease while driving. On a circuit, I rarely feel in any danger, while on the rally I didn't feel safe at all!

The difference between a racer and a rallyman

I think rally drivers need many extra qualities above and beyond what we have. You can become a good circuit racer quite quickly, which I don't think is possible in rallying. You don't just suddenly become a rally driver; it takes time to learn the job, a lot more than it takes a racing driver. The element of experience is essential, and it doesn't surprise me that the great rally champions are generally a fair bit older than us!

TESTING AND
SETTING UP

Between driving theory and the reality of a race, the setting up of a chassis has grown and grown in importance over the last 15 years or so.

Today, it's no longer enough simply to drive quickly and well. You also have to be capable of understanding the car, analysing its behaviour, and finding ways of perfecting the set-up. A superb driver at the wheel of a badly sorted car will be less competitive than a run-of-the-mill driver in a car that has been set up perfectly. Similarly, the difference between two equally matched drivers will eventually come down to how their car has been adjusted to suit a particular event.

Less important in bygone days, this modern phenomenon is due to the fact that a contemporary racing car has a multitude of parameters that mechanics and engineers can adjust from one extreme to the other. With clear understanding of potential problems, sound technical feedback and a good feeling for test driving, a driver can fully exploit his car's potential. Misunderstanding or vague interpretations of a car's behaviour will send you in the opposite direction. The car won't be set up correctly, which will lead to further complications, and it won't be used to its maximum effect.

TESTING AND PRACTICE

There are two sorts, both very different in nature: private testing and official practice.

■ Private testing

This takes place on a circuit, where you seek to improve the performance and handling of your car, and is often limited according to how much you can afford to do. There are three main types of private testing.

The first involves visiting a new circuit to prepare for an event taking place in the future. This gives the driver a chance to learn the track and work out a few reference points, while thinking all the time about the set-up he is likely to need for the race.

The second kind is more akin to routine work: running in engines and gearboxes, bedding in brakes, while simultaneously checking that all the main systems are functioning normally.

The third category is the most important, being that where you work to improve the car with an eye on its performance in the long term. At the top level, this work involves leading engineers; at the amateur level, you might just take one mechanic along with you. There are an infinite number of possibilities when it comes to car development. Initiative, intelligence and imagination will always provide fresh solutions. Realistically, the limit to what you can achieve is likely to be dictated by financial considerations!

THE MÉJANES ESSES AT FRANCE'S LE CASTELLET CIRCUIT

This series of bends, situated just after the start of Le Castellet's short circuit, provides a first-class illustration of how theory can differ from practice.

Firstly, drivers must brake for the opening corner while steering, i.e. with the majority of the car's mass on the two left-hand wheels. A classic braking manoeuvre at the end of the straight before turning in would result in too great a time-loss and a waste of the velocity built up along the preceding straight.

Efficiency through the initial right-hander is partially sacrificed. At best, the car will find

itself on the median line, i.e. in the middle of the track, on exit. As for the following left, it is totally sacrificed in order to increase exit speed from the final right-hander leading onto the Mistral Straight.

This series of three bends demands a specific approach which should have exit speed from the final element as its principal objective. The example of the Méjanes Esses clearly demonstrates how the ideal line through a corner is always a product of the latter's overall context.

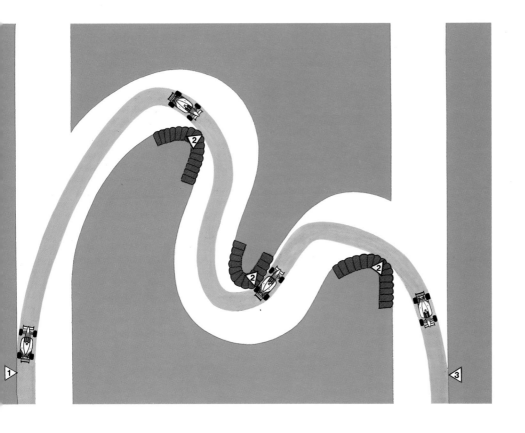

Private testing can play a major role in the success or otherwise of a team. Out of the limelight, a great deal of development work can be completed in preparation for the season ahead.

■ Official practice

This is much more strictly controlled than testing, and doesn't give you as much time, taking place two or three days before a race (although at amateur level, it might be on the morning of the event). There is always a chance to try something new during practice, but the main thing is to concentrate on adapting the car to the nature of the circuit.

During official practice, cars' lap times are recorded, which has a bearing on the race as your best lap time determines your position on the starting grid. And the higher you are up the grid – pole position if possible – the better your prospects in the race.

In major events, there will also be untimed practice, which gives drivers much-needed time to set up their cars. That should only be a question of fine tuning, as the bulk of the work should be done in the close-season, or between races.

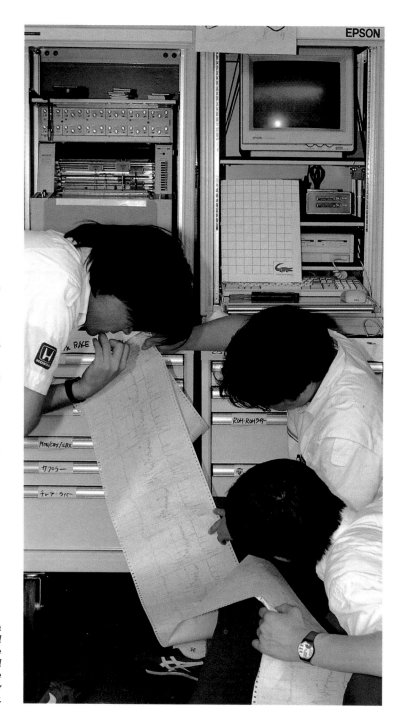

During testing, computers record data concerning not only the chassis (roll, lateral grip, suspension travel...) but also the engine (temperatures, pressures, engine speed, fuel consumption...). Afterwards, engineers analyse the print-outs and make any necessary adjustments to the car.

VARIOUS ADJUSTMENTS

Racing car manufacturers provide customers with a guide to basic settings, which it is best to stick to rigorously. The settings may vary a little from car to car, but they provide a sound reference point, and a mechanic should need only a couple of days in the workshop to follow the manufacturer's guidelines to the letter.

This preliminary work is invaluable. It should be carried out on a new car before it turns a wheel. Regular checks should then be made to confirm that nothing has gone awry during use, particularly after an accident. In any case, the car should be inspected as often as possible.

In this chapter, we must differentiate between drivers at the three different levels of motor sport:

– the amateur, who buys his car and only has himself and perhaps a mechanic on hand to prepare and race it; other than following the advice supplied by the manufacturer, he has no real resources;
– the semi-professional, who doesn't buy the car, which belongs to a team; he has several mechanics, and maybe an engineer, all of whom know perfectly well how to set up and prepare the car, so that the driver can leave most of it up to them;
– the professional, who doesn't deal with a manufacturer, but rather directly with the design-engineer who conceived and created the car, perhaps even with a particular driver in mind.

For amateurs, there are several stages involved in setting up a chassis. The two most important are the standard settings (mainly mechanical, as recommended by the manufacturer or engineer who designed the car; indispensible, they should be checked over regularly in the workshop), and the dynamic settings (both mechanical and aerodynamic, which are used to adapt a car for a particular event, and should therefore be done on site).

■ Static settings

These aim to achieve a perfect weight distribution throughout the car. They also allow perfect symmetry and complete respect for all the guidelines laid down by the manufacturer, in the different areas which we will study in detail.

Several methods can be used: plumb line, metal rods or optical beams. In all cases, you must use perfectly straight axes to measure the settings. And it is most important to work on a totally flat surface. At the highest levels of the sport, teams carry a perfectly horizontal, rectangular plate with them. The car can be set up on this at any circuit throughout the world.

This transportable flat surface allows engineers to set up the car on a perfectly level plane. In this way, identical settings can be reproduced in the pits of circuits the world over.

Tyres

The first precaution is to check that the pressure is correct. It is also necessary to ensure that the tyres all have the same circumference. Such variations are possible in manufacture, and the tiniest difference can unsettle a car under acceleration or at high speed. The best solution is to use steel wheels, very thin and barely larger than those on a bicycle. They replicate the dimensions of the tyres perfectly, without being subject to any deformation. You can thus work more thoroughly and take more exact measurements.

Anti-roll bars

The second precaution is to disconnect the anti-roll bars front and rear, in order to release the suspension. You can thus check that it moves freely without either side being subject to greater tension than the other.

Ground clearance

If, for example, a manufacturer recommends 5 cm ground clearance at the front and 6 cm at the rear, you place blocks of exactly those heights underneath the car at the relevant points. They should fit perfectly without being forced (which would indicate that the car was running

Alain Prost: 'In order to set the ride height as accurately as possible, I stay in the car to "make up the weight". Engineers have also taken the precaution of replacing the rubber tyres with metal wheels. Today's Formula 1 cars run very low, with the flat bottom extremely close to the surface of the track. That's why sparks can often be seen coming from the rear over small bumps. A variation in ground clearance of plus or minus 1 millimetre, especially at the front, can make a big difference to the aerodynamic qualities of the car and, therefore, its overall efficiency.'

Opposite: Benetton's tyre man checks pressures on arrival at the circuit.

too low) if the car is running with the specified ground clearance.

Castor angle

This is another measurement supplied by the manufacturer, principally concerning the front wheels. Castor gives greater responsiveness and stability to the front wheels. The larger the castor angle, the heavier the steering and the more stable the front end.

Alternatively, the less castor angle you run, the lighter the steering becomes and the more lively the car will be entering a corner.

Tyre specialists are forever taking temperature readings. Measurements are taken at three different points (outside, middle and inside) of the tyre's surface. The ideal working temperature is in the region of 90°C to 110°C.

Camber angles

Camber angles range from zero to several degrees negative. Camber is designed to make a tyre work as effectively as possible when a car is loaded up in a corner.

At rest, you apply negative camber so that a tyre will have optimal contact with the road when fully stressed, i.e. that it will be as close to perpendicular as possible. Confirmation that a tyre is being used effectively can be obtained by checking the temperature of the tread. If it's too hot on the inside, it indicates that the camber angle is too great, and that the contact patch is not evenly distributed across the tyre. If it's insufficiently warm, it usually indicates insufficient camber, although in this case other factors can also come into play.

Toe-in/Toe-out

When a car is set at a specific ground clearance, it is adjusted perfectly. But as soon as it shifts on its front suspension – either dropping down under braking or rising under acceleration – 'induced steering' results. Among other things, adjustments to toe-in/toe-out are designed to counteract these distortions.

At the front, the location of the

As Nelson Piquet quenches his thirst during private testing at Monza, engineers check front toe-in by means of a light beam which reflects off a special rule laid on the ground.

Special electronic scales permanently indicate the load on each corner. By modifying suspension and ground clearance, the weight borne by each wheel can be adjusted up or down.

steering rack is crucial, and it should be adjusted so that the steering arms don't affect the movement of the suspension.

Toe-in/toe-out modifications therefore control and restrict 'induced steering'.

Weight distribution

In order to distribute weight accurately, it's best to install the driver in the car – failing that, put an equivalent weight in the cockpit – and to make sure that the fuel tanks are at least half full. You can check on the scales that there is a perfect balance

between the left and right wheels, front and rear. The margins of tolerance are very low. Note that persistent locking of a front wheel under braking will upset the weight distribution.

Ensuring correct general alignment

It is possible that the front and rear wheels will be correctly adjusted in relation to the chassis, but that doesn't mean that they will be in alignment with each other. It is always worth checking to make sure that both sets of wheels are on the same axis.

■ Dynamic settings

This covers two subjects which are at the same time distinct yet closely interconnected: aerodynamic and mechanical adjustments. The first apply to everything which affects the airflow over the car: the front wing, the single- or double-plane rear wing, trim tabs and bodywork. Beyond such aerodynamic aids, these adjustments also take into account the way the car sits on the road, whether it is raised or lowered at the front, for example. There are two ways of calculating the correct level of what is known as 'downforce'.

It is best first to balance the car. You don't want it to grip at the front but not at the rear, or vice versa.

Secondly, it is necessary to adjust the whole car according to the nature of the circuit, all the while bearing in mind the balance front to rear.

The more downforce you put on a car, the better it holds the road, but the slower it will be in a straight line. Alternatively, reduce the downforce and the car will be less efficient in corners, but quicker on the straight. Once again, it is necessary to find a suitable compromise, as you can't hope to have the best of both worlds.

Aerodynamics represent a vital part of modern racing. The concept first appeared in the late Sixties, and it has had a profound effect on the sport ever since.

Mechanical adjustments take into account all the suspension components: springs, dampers bump-stops and anti-roll bars. This has always been a classic part of race car tuning. In spite of its importance, it has rather been overtaken in recent years by aerodynamic influences, the more so since speeds have become higher and higher. Put simply, such mechanical adjustments are still critical up to a certain point. Generally, problems occurring at around 60–75 mph can be dialled out through suspension tuning. Any faster, and the solution will probably lie in an aerodynamic adjustment. To a degree, you can also camouflage the effects of inadequate suspension settings by having the car aerodynamically perfect.

But while a mistake with aerodynamic set-up will carry virtually no penalty at low speed, you cannot hope to correct such a problem at high speed by adjusting the suspension.

What can be done about understeer?

If a car understeers too much, that is it lacks frontal grip, there are

The design of a car's front and rear wings, as well as the body itself, is aimed at achieving aerodynamic downforce.

The steeper the angle of the front wings, the more downforce keeps the front end 'glued' to the track. This could help overcome a problem with understeer or, in extreme cases, might purposely be done to provoke oversteer.

several possible remedial adjustments.

Mechanical

Excessive understeer could be a result of having the front springs, dampers and/or anti-roll bar set too hard, or alternatively the rear springs, dampers and/or anti-roll bar set too soft.

Aerodynamic

Understeer in a fast corner might be the result of insufficient frontal downforce, or possibly too much rear downforce. The same effect can be produced by running the car too high at the front/too low at the rear, as that also affects the airflow around the bodywork.

Tyres

Incorrect tyre pressures can also cause understeer, in any type of corner. Under-inflation will cause the front tyres to overheat through being too soft; over-inflation will prevent them getting up to working temperature, resulting in a loss of grip.

And oversteer?

If a car has a tendency to oversteer, that is for the rear tyres to break away prematurely, you have to draw a distinction between fast and slow corners. Then follow the same rules as you would to counter an understeer problem (i.e. adjustments to suspension, aerodynamics or tyres), albeit the other way round (so you might add downforce to the rear wing to counter fast-corner oversteer).

It can happen that no amount of fine tuning will rid the car of its basic oversteering or understeering attitude. In that

The rear wing fills the same function at the rear, as well as playing the additional role of increasing ground effect by accelerating the evacuation of air under the car. However, excessive downforce at the rear might penalise a car's top speed along the straights.

case, it's a good idea deliberately to reduce the efficiency of one part of the car in favour of the other, to see if that makes it any easier to drive. So, in the case of excessive understeer, you might reduce the level of rear-end grip. In the end, the stop-watch is more likely than the driver to decide which is the best compromise.

While setting up a car during test sessions, a driver must also check his brake balance regularly, make wholesale adjustments if it rains and adapt gear ratios to suit the different layout of each racing circuit.

■ Brake Balance

Weight transfer under braking puts more strain on the front of the car, so it is always best to have more brake bias at the front than at the rear.

Setting up in the workshop
With the car jacked up, one party turns the wheels while another brakes progressively harder.

As soon as the front wheels start to feel the effects of the brakes, the ideal is to have the rear wheels just starting to slow down. At all costs, you should avoid having the rear wheels braking before the fronts. It's acceptable to have them braking at the same time. Then, you should just increase the frontal bias by a couple of notches.

Setting up at the circuit
To discover the state of your brake balance in a hurry, you should simply press hard on the pedal to provoke lock-up. At first, this should be done at a modest speed down the straight, then a little bit faster and even in mid-corner if need be. But clearly you shouldn't take the slightest risk, and it should be done in such a way that you always maintain full control.

If a front wheel locks, you will feel a gentle judder through the steering wheel at the moment when, having relaxed the pedal, the tyres regrip. In a straight line, that will be the only tell-tale if you can't actually see the front wheels. On the other hand, it's easy to detect going into a corner. Firstly, the car will start to understeer. Then, when you release the brakes, the front wheels will react more sharply than your steering input suggests they should.

If the rear wheels lock up on the

as aerodynamic downforce and weight distribution will be affected. In this case, it is naturally better to ensure that the car is set up to favour high-speed deceleration.

■ The effects of rain

Mechanical adjustments

The settings on which you started out should be softened all round with regard to spring rates, shock absorbers and anti-roll bars. It might even be worth

New brake pads must be bedded in before they are totally effective. Drivers are able to adjust front–rear brake balance themselves, while technicians ensure that the discs are operating at optimum working temperature, between 400°C and 600°C. Small heat-sensitive tabs applied to the brakes during testing change colour according to maximum temperature reached. Depending upon the result, technicians can increase or reduce cooling airflow to the discs to achieve the ideal temperature.

straight, the car becomes unstable. It tries to wriggle around, and might go sideways. Again, these reactions will be accentuated if the exercise is tried in mid-corner.

If a front-wheel-drive car locks its front wheels (or a RWD car its rears), you may notice a momentary loss of power, or possibly even a complete cut-out. This is because the locked wheels have a direct link with the engine.

Finally, perfect brake balance at modest speed won't necessarily be as effective at higher speeds,

disconnecting the rear anti-roll bar altogether in order to obtain better traction. It is equally possible that you might detach the front roll bar in order to balance an understeering car, while leaving the rear one connected but on its softest setting.

Where possible, springs and shock absorbers should be softened off in equal measure front and rear.

Aerodynamic adjustments

As grip is considerably reduced by the rain, it is logical to look for greater downforce. Thus you should run more front and rear wing, while at the same time trying to maintain the overall balance of the car.

Braking adjustments

The slippery surface reduces the grip of the front wheels, thus producing a slight weight transfer to the rear. Without touching the brake balance, the front wheels will thus start to lock up. To avoid that, turn the brake balance a couple of notches to the rear, to restore equilibrium. Then, as the track gradually dries out, progressively increase the frontal bias so that you revert to the original set-up when the circuit is fully dry.

■ Gearing

In motor sport, a gearbox can be taken apart in minutes. It is therefore simple to adjust the gearing to suit the nature of the circuit you are lapping.

Top gear

This is the ratio which will be used on the fastest parts of the

circuit. It should therefore allow the engine to operate at the top of the power curve. Thus the ratio you might use at a circuit where the top speed is 125 mph is markedly different to that you would use when travelling at 175 mph. If maximum power is at 9000 rpm, you don't want to be at either 8500 rpm or 9500 rpm when travelling flat out. In the first instance, the driver has his foot hard down but there are no more revs available. Top gear (fifth or sixth, depending on the type of gearbox) is thus too long and needs to be shortened by 500 rpm so that the engine can operate at its 9000 rpm peak.

In the second, top gear is too short, and the driver will eventually over-rev the engine

Beyond the special chassis settings required for wet-weather racing, the driver's role in such conditions is crucial. A keen sense of balance, a quick all-encompassing eye and precise movements at the wheel are qualities which every driver who excels in the rain possesses.

There are any number of reasons why gear ratios might have to be modified: a car might have been made heavier by a full tank of fuel; the fitting of qualifying tyres might allow some corners to be taken quicker during practice; technicians might have set revised engine rev limits; the direction of the wind might have changed; engineers might have set more or less aerodynamic downforce, etc, etc.

without the car being able to go any faster. And unless he has a rev-limiter fitted it might just blow up...

The minimum difference between two gear cogs should be around 200–300 rpm, which isn't much. The driver thus has to take several other things into account when selecting his top gear: the strength and direction of the wind can change from one day to the next; the likelihood of slipstreaming, which is more common in a race, when cars are together, than it is in qualifying; whether or not you are running on full tanks, which constitutes a weight disadvantage; the aerodynamic set-up of the car, which affects straightline speed; the favourable (or not) slope on the main straights (in which case you concentrate on the uphill parts, lifting off if need be on the downhill stretch). So you can see why mechanics often change gear ratios in between qualifying and racing.

First gear

First gear is sometimes used for a particularly tight corner – such as a hairpin – but generally circuit speeds are so high that it is never used once the race is under way.

Thus you choose first gear purely for the start of the race. If the start/finish straight is flat, you will use the same ratio from one circuit to the next. But if the start is on a slight incline it is better to use a shorter ratio, and similarly to use a longer one if the grid faces downhill.

Choosing the other gears

The best gear in which to take a given corner is one you can hold all the way through. It is important that the driver should not have to change gear before the exit, or even just after. Ideally, the driver should hold one gear all the way through a corner and attain peak power in the first few yards of the subsequent straight: thus you change up when the car is totally stable.

The spacing of the intermediate gears

Generally, the gearing should be as close as possible, and there shouldn't be any 'gaps' between ratios, so that the engine remains in operation between its maximum torque and peak power. If the peculiar nature of a circuit necessitates lengthening – or shortening – a ratio to the detriment of the ideal balance, it's least damaging in the lower gears, as the car is travelling more slowly when you shift from second to third than when you go from fifth to sixth. Any compromise should be directed therefore at the lower gears, but given the choice between 'too short' and 'too long' you should always go for the second: that will be less wearing on the engine, and will allow you to corner more quickly as you won't be slowed either by an over-revving engine or the need to change gear in mid-corner.

It is essential that a driver has gear ratios appropriate to the circumstances and the characteristics of the circuit. It is a simple matter for a mechanic to change the ratios to meet a driver's requirements, as modern racing gearboxes can be dismantled in minutes.

The green button allows radio contact with the pits while the red one, during the turbo era in F1, permitted drivers to increase boost from the cockpit with a view to facilitating overtaking. To the right, the small gearshift requires little travel so as to lose the least time possible when changing gear. The linear rev-counter can be spotted just above the steering wheel, tucked in below the windscreen.

ANALYSING A CAR'S RESPONSES

■ The main points

Before looking at how a driver should analyse the responses and handling of his car, it is worth recalling some of the principles which usually govern test sessions. Concerning the car first of all, it will behave very differently depending on whether it's on a public road or a circuit. In the first case, you're looking for manageability and sharp reactions, i.e. a responsive front end producing a tendency to oversteer. In the second, you're after high-speed stability and good traction coming out of bends, in other words an effective rear end promoting natural understeer. For rallies, the ideal is a car that isn't too difficult to handle in quick corners, while for circuits the driver wants a car that he can coax into understeer whenever he thinks it necessary...

In this pursuit of perfect handling, it is essential to take a look at the behaviour and style of the driver himself. You can divide drivers into just two groups. The first contains those who like a car to oversteer: you find here all those who turn in and accelerate late, hurl their car onto the racing line to make it slide, then control it via the throttle and opposite lock.

The second group prefer an understeering car: generally, they turn in and get onto the power early, ease gently onto the racing line and do their best to stop the car sliding. So perhaps you can now see how two cars, belonging to the same team, might be set up very differently at the same circuit in accordance with the different styles of two drivers. And it's thus unsurprising that one driver should be slower than the other after an impromptu car swap.

■ Analysis of a corner

In addition to the simple distinction between fast and slow corners, it is worthwhile looking in detail at a car's reactions through each of the three parts comprising any bend. For this,

The way a chassis turns into a corner tells the driver a great deal about its general behaviour and balance. A chassis is said to be 'lazy' when it reacts poorly to a command from the steering wheel, 'lively' when the front wheels respond to the slightest steering correction.

we'll describe the behaviour of a typical (i.e. rear-wheel-drive) circuit racer. Many of the points are also common to front- and four-wheel-drive cars in other events.

Entry

At the entry to a slow corner, the car is decelerating, and all the weight is transferred to the front. The problem is to get the car swiftly onto the racing line. The driver should pay attention to several responses: 'Will it go where the steering wheel tells it to? Isn't it feeling a little sluggish?'

Entering a fast corner, the car will be accelerating. It shouldn't be committed too sharply to the racing line, nor should there be too much understeer. 'How will it turn in? Is there more or less grip at the front than there was during the last few laps, before I pitted to adjust the suspension?'

Mid-corner

In the middle of a slow corner, the throttle can influence the behaviour of the rear wheels in a number of ways. The driver can wait a little longer before accelerating; he can also apply either light or heavy pressure to the pedal. Whatever, he will be able to assess the instability of the rear end. 'Is it sliding a little, a lot or far too much?'

In the middle of a quick corner, the weight is transferred to the outside of the car, and with the power already on hard you have to be able to detect the state of the car's balance. 'Are all four wheels sliding? Or is it just the fronts? Is there enough lateral grip? Is the rear end breaking away too much?'

Exit

At the exit of a slow corner, under hard acceleration, the main problem could be poor traction, if the weight transfer to the rear wheels is in some way deficient. 'Is the inside rear wheel spinning? Is the rear end breaking away at all?'

The driver opposite-locks as the rear end slides out and flirts with the kerb, the painted surface of which has been rendered slippery by the rain...

At the exit of a quick corner, the driver should notice gentle understeer, which he can induce via a gentle movement of the throttle pedal. 'Is the car understeering too much? Will it snap into oversteer if I lift off?'

■ The influence of the driver

To analyse correctly a car's reactions, you have to bear in mind the manner in which it is

This amount of oversteer out of a corner is never easy to contend with. When the rear tyres find grip again, the chassis might well react by brutally sending the rear sliding in the opposite direction. A poorly set-up chassis, worn tyres or too much power are the most common reasons for such behaviour.

being driven. Remember that a skilled driver will be able to provoke the same car into either oversteer or understeer in the same corner, simply by changing his driving technique. So, aside from your own driving style, which you should preserve at all costs, you must consider a whole series of small mistakes which might affect a car's behaviour.

And that can lead to incorrect adjustments in the pits, the product of decisions made on a false premiss.

So, during the first few laps of a circuit, at the start of a test session, it isn't unusual to brake too soon for a corner, to find yourself going too slowly as you turn in and thus to accelerate prematurely: the car will understeer on the exit as a result...

Conversely, a spirited driver has a natural predilection for late braking which endows him with a certain harshness at the wheel and obliges him to accelerate relatively late in the corner: there is thus a strong likelihood of oversteer in mid-corner...

These driving styles are clumsy, and if the driver doesn't pull his socks up he will pit and demand unsuitable adjustments, having mixed up cause and effect. This confusion leads to familiar situations. A driver pits and complains of excessive oversteer at the exit of medium-speed corners, yet there is a strong chance that the car is set up with understeer characteristics and any subsequent changes will achieve the opposite of the desired effect! This happens when an understeering car is unresponsive entering a corner and the driver, having failed to spot it, thinks that he didn't turn the wheel enough. So next time

the driver turns too much, the car understeers all the way through the bend and the back end breaks away towards the exit. This type of oversteer is difficult to catch as it is brutal, and the driver will be kept busy at the wheel as he recovers from excessive steering input to a position of opposite lock.

Generally, remember that there is no point turning the wheel too far. Beyond a certain angle this simply provokes understeer as you ask too much of the front tyres. And if engineers design steering racks allowing greater movement of the front wheels, it is purely to facilitate the application of opposite lock in difficult conditions (such as rain, oil or on flecks of rubber).

In conclusion, a good driver will analyse his car's reactions accurately if he is aware of his own precision, or lack of it: did he turn the wheel too early or too late, gently or forcibly? Did he release the brake pedal before or after the turn-in point? Was he progressive or brutal on the throttle? Did he regain control early or late?

OFFICIAL PRACTICE

Electric cells give instant and accurate data concerning speeds at different parts of the circuit, allowing teams to optimise their chassis settings by establishing a better compromise between the slower and faster parts of the track.

During official practice, drivers have two objectives, which don't necessarily depend on the same set of chassis parameters. The first is to look for pure speed, in a bid to secure the best possible place on the starting grid. Among the difficulties faced here, we'll examine qualifying tyres and the problems created by slower cars later on.

The second objective is to find a decent chassis set-up for the race itself, which implies different settings. In seeking these eventual improvements, the driver has at his disposal:

1 – his senses: the reactions and handling of the car should be up to their normal efficiency and suit his style of driving so that he feels completely at ease;
2 – timing equipment: over a complete lap of the circuit, this will give him an overall picture; over certain sections of the circuit, it can provide more detailed information. The relative

performances of drivers through a given corner can be timed in hundredths of a second, and allow the driver to see where he is losing out or making up time on his rivals.

■Qualifying tyres

Teams will stop at nothing when it comes to improving tyre performance. Special tyre warmers allow the rubber to reach ideal working temperatures before they are fitted.

During timed practice, drivers use soft-compound qualifying tyres, which have a useful life of just two or three laps. This is characteristic of all qualifying tyres, while even race tyres –

designed to do a full race distance – will produce their best performance during their first few laps. After a certain time, which varies according to the compound (although it's rarely more than four or five laps), their efficiency diminishes progressively. To begin with you lose a second or two per lap, but this eventually stabilises without in any way compromising either reliability or driver safety.

This situation demands certain things of the driver in qualifying. When the car is set up correctly, when all necessary changes have been made, when the driver has learnt all he can about the circuit, he knows he only has a couple of laps in which to give his best. It's up to him to concentrate, quickly and hard, so that he is capable of getting straight into his rhythm as soon as he leaves the pits, in order to set a time by his third lap at the latest. Beyond that, there is no sense carrying on. There is little point driving a perfect lap when the tyres have lost their edge to the tune of over one second per lap. This modern breed of tyre obliges drivers to produce a totally committed effort over a very short period of time during qualifying sessions.

■ Dealing with traffic

One of the principal hazards encountered by drivers during qualifying sessions is traffic moving at a variety of different speeds, with a lot of pit stops being made. It is thus the responsibility of each driver to spot a suitable moment to go for a time: to notice when there are comparatively few cars on the circuit in order to run the least risk of being balked. It's a matter of experience, and sometimes of luck.

Traffic can be a real problem during qualifying. Real and dangerous, in that drivers are extracting the maximum from their cars at a time when other competitors may be cruising. In such situations, it is vital that drivers use their mirrors out of respect for others, if they themselves want to be respected: if, by going too slowly, they block a fast-moving rival, they will sooner or later get a taste of their own medicine,

Without the goodwill and understanding of fellow-drivers, it is exceedingly difficult to get a 'clear run' during qualifying, i.e. a lap where time hasn't been lost as a result of a slower driver who does not get out of the way immediately.

intentionally or otherwise...

There has to be understanding between drivers who are, after all, supposed to be responsible. More than simple courtesy and fair play, it's a matter of ethics. When a driver is travelling quickly, he has to concentrate upon what he's doing. If going slowly, he should therefore try to make life easier for those who wish to pass.

■ The difference between practice and race settings

At first sight, it may seem paradoxical to do away with the settings that enabled you to set your fastest qualifying lap before the race.

This difference between qualifying and race set-ups is all the more marked if the circuit features extremely fast sections (a very long straight, for example).

That would mean looking for grip in practice, to ensure greater pace in the slow sections of the circuit at the expense of straightline speed. For the race,

you'd look to achieve the opposite effect.

The reason is simple. It's all a question of tactics, and the ability to pass your rivals in the race. Being slower in the tight sections is no great penalty, because it is not easy for other drivers to pass you there, and by going off line to attempt a passing manoeuvre they'd be taking a chance. And on the straight, you'd have the advantage so long as your car was adjusted correctly.

Conversely, being quicker in the corners isn't always an advantage. Greater efficiency doesn't make overtaking any easier, and you can often lose a lot of time before a suitable overtaking opportunity – which can be a delicate matter in mid-corner – presents itself.

This phenomenon is certainly not true of all circuits. At a sinuous track like Monaco, for instance, qualifying and race settings will be more or less the same.

WHAT MAKES A GOOD TEST DRIVER?

Despite the development of electronics and the increasing presence of computers at race meetings, a driver's first impressions at the end of a practice session are a vital source of information for engineers.

Modern motor sport places considerable demands on its champions. They must be capable of complete mastery of their car, of driving it quickly and additionally of perceiving what is happening around them at all levels. Even if they aren't asked to engineer the car, their role consists of taking note of the car's various reactions all around the circuit, and explaining them in exact detail when they get back to the pits. Normally, they won't have to throw in possible technical and aerodynamic solutions to any problems encountered.

So even an excellent driver can't do absolutely everything at once. Responsibilities should be allocated to different members of the team, each of whom should carry them out to the best of his abilities. One of the hazards facing young drivers is the difficulty of creating an organised infrastructure out of nothing. And when there is only one mechanic, as is often the case, the driver can find himself seriously overburdened. This can have unfortunate results. It is much better that a driver should concentrate on his car's handling. It's up to the technicians to interpret his feedback and carry out the appropriate adjustments.

The importance of the driver's role in setting up a car can never be stressed enough. To assess the success or otherwise of any modifications they have effected, engineers have to rely on what the driver tells them.

■ Having a 'feel' for the car

Traditionally, drivers have been divided into two groups. One features those who need a car to be set up perfectly in order for them to go quickly, the other those who are labelled 'natural' drivers. No matter how their car is set up, the latter are apparently able to lap quickly at will. They compensate for their slight lack of technical ability by driving around any problems which ensue. That's no bad thing in motor racing. Such a driver will obtain excellent results at the wheel of a car set up by someone else, but sooner or later in his career he will find himself held back. Even if he continues to drive quickly, he will eventually encounter two big problems as a result of his inability to interpret exactly what the car is doing.

The first arises from his difficulty in adapting a car to the demands of a specific circuit. This can mean less gifted rivals proving themselves more effective.

The second has long-term consequences for the car's overall development programme. Improvements usually come as the result of continual technical progress made race by race. If a driver is unable to do this, he risks – without being aware of it – slowly but surely eroding the car's full potential.

Under the watchful eye of an engineer, mechanics bend over the innards of their machine to satisfy Stefan Johansson's request for an adjustment to the front spring rates.

■ Consistency

To assist in the process of setting a car up for a circuit, a driver has to use all his powers of concentration. First of all, he has to tackle each corner in three stages, as previously described. Then, once he has established reference points and the correct racing line, he should try to stick to them as closely as possible. Varying the line from one lap to the next alters a car's behaviour and creates extra problems. As soon as a driver has got to grips with a circuit, he should be able to complete a lap in the same fashion time after time. If each lap follows the same pattern, the driver is better able to analyse events objectively. Indeed, such consistency makes the driver a reference point in himself. This requires much attention to detail, but by maintaining the same procedure for lap after lap you become a good test driver.

■ Objectivity

The last essential asset for a good test driver is objectivity. A driver must not believe, because such and such a thing is being changed on his car, that it will necessarily bring about an improvement. It is better to find out by analysing the situation objectively, rather than trusting theory and convincing yourself that such an adjustment is for the best. Besides, in the cold light of day the stop-watch will tell you the facts.

Astute team managers might not always keep a young novice informed about changes made to his car, for the aforementioned reasons. Being in the dark, not knowing about modifications and the lap times which result from them, is mighty difficult. The driver gets the terrible impression that he is permanently under someone else's wing. His only escape is thus to double his concentration and focus his attention purely on the car's responses: 'Here, it's understeering, which it didn't before. Well less, anyway. There, it's breaking away more quickly at the rear, whereas on the previous lap...'

Clear, calm and collected analysis is vital for a good test driver, who has to show not only that he can drive quickly, but also that he understands the car.

All the perplexity of a champion betrayed by his machine can be read here in René Arnoux's expression. Driver experience and talent are not hard and fast guarantees of results.

Alain Prost's comments

The first few laps

Whenever I take a car out for the very first time, I do a couple of gentle laps of the circuit at most, just to make sure that everything works properly, easing through the gears and so forth. Then the mechanics check the engine to ensure that there are no oil or water leaks. So whenever you take a car out for the first time, it's simply to check that all systems are in working order. You don't go straight out to set quick lap times. You chisel away at that later.

If a car is good straight out of the box, the driver should be able to tell almost immediately. After no more than ten laps, I already know whether or not a car is up to scratch. Having left the workshop, the best cars will set competitive lap times almost straight away. That's because aerodynamics play such an important part with modern racing cars, and much of the development work is done in the wind tunnel. If you've got a good aerodynamicist, the car should – on paper at least – be on the pace. Once on the track, it's just a question of balancing it front and rear. As far as suspension is concerned, engineers are always coming up with new sketches, but we've seen most of them before! Suspension is used more today to control the attitude of the car in the interests of aerodynamic downforce.

How a young driver should make adjustments

To start with, the first thing a beginner should do, as far as setting up his car is concerned, is to complete as many laps as possible without worrying about other drivers. He must try to learn all about the car, systematically changing key components to see how they affect it: try a different anti-roll bar, softer then harder springs, adjust the aerodynamic downforce, that sort of thing. Even in the junior formulae, driving skill alone is not enough, so you must know how to get the most from your chassis. At that level, you can probably gain a second per lap through skilful driving, but lose three times as much by setting the car up incorrectly.

Learning a circuit

When you get to a new circuit for the first time, it's always worth doing a lap on foot and then, if possible, in a saloon car. The latter will give you quite a different perspective from that you'll get when walking, and it'll change again when you lap in a single-seater. During this reconnaissance, make a note of any distinguishing marks: the quality of the track surface (bumpy or even, abrasive or smooth), the nature of the circuit (tight and twisty, fast or somewhere in between), and the type of set-up that you are likely to need. In this respect, it is usual to start out with an excess of aerodynamic downforce, and to adjust it as appropriate if necessary: that makes the car more predictable during your first few laps.

It is also worth studying the run-off areas, particularly in the quicker corners (sand-traps, catch-fencing, grass), the angle and position of the guard rails, and the height of the kerbs. Check the latter carefully: if they are too high, it would be dangerous to run over them; if they are low enough, don't hesitate to use them!

Mechanical adjustments

Firstly, always heat up your tyres sufficiently, so that you can set representative lap times which enable you to evaluate the car more accurately. Then you can work on springs, dampers and bump-stops. You can never be sure that such and such a setting will work better. All you can do is try it and see. Even then, this type of adjustment might not produce a definitive solution. For instance, a different spring rating can give you more grip front or rear. But by changing the stiffness of the springs, you are also altering the car's aerodynamic balance. Whether you fit harder or softer springs, you will modify it in some way. So it is generally best to stick to the principle that everything has to be checked to ensure that you have the optimum set-up on the car.

Aerodynamic adjustments

Before even thinking about modifying a car's set-up, I find it essential to establish exactly how much aerodynamic downforce it needs. You can't touch the suspension without having this information to hand. You will need more or less downforce depending on whether the circuit is fast or slow. This is something that becomes easier to determine with experience, on the part of both the engineer who designed the car and, in particular, the driver. You should know after two or three laps whether or not you're running enough, and to avoid possible mistakes it's better to opt for too much than not enough.

In my opinion, aerodynamic downforce is the hub of setting up a car. Once you've got that right, you can work on the rest.

If you go the other way, you'll be all at sea. If a driver hasn't found a good aerodynamic set-up for the car, he'll be banging his head against a brick wall no matter what he changes (springs, roll bars, dampers). So you must be absolutely sure that your aerodynamics are sound before all else: firstly as far as downforce is concerned, and then balance, to make sure that you've neither too much understeer nor too much oversteer. Only then can you start to consider adjustments to anything else.

The effect of the anti-roll bars

The more you stiffen up the front suspension, whether via the anti-roll bars or the springs, the more the front wheels will have a tendency to lose their grip. On the other hand, because the front wheels are stable, there will be less roll, which puts more weight onto the inside rear wheel, which is thus less likely to break away. Thus you reduce the likelihood of the wheel spinning at the expense of traction. But, as ever, you have to find a compromise between what you've lost (i.e. frontal grip) and what you've gained. It's often said that stiffening the front bar has the same effect as slackening off the rear, which isn't strictly true, even if the end result is more or less the same. Whatever, you should aim to have minimum chassis roll while losing as little grip as possible.

Spring stiffness

No matter what type of circuit you are on, aerodynamics take precedence in F1 nowadays. With flat-bottomed cars, you want to avoid changing the way they 'sit' on the circuit. Thus, in the interests of aerodynamic consistency, we use very stiff springs. Generally, the more aerodynamic downforce you run, the harder the springs should be. But even in low-downforce mode we use comparatively stiff springs. That certainly costs a little grip in tight bends. But it is of vital importance that downforce remains constant in faster corners.

Perfect handling

My driving style is best suited by an F1 car which handles neutrally as you turn in, and then has a gentle tendency to understeer as you accelerate out of the corner. But achieving such a set-up is rare indeed! Despite my best efforts, I sometimes have to drive cars which are very nervous, bordering on oversteer. They are still efficient, and I manage in spite of my driving style. But that doesn't change the fact that the aforementioned handling characteristics are more effective.

Tyre temperatures

Of course, it is always best to have an even spread of temperature over each tyre, ideally between 75°C minimum and 105–110°C maximum. I'm not sure whether it's down to modern tyres or the present-day cars, but you tend either to find a set of tyres with perfectly balanced temperatures, or a set that aren't balanced at all! In the latter case, any number of changes to toe-in or camber appear to make little difference. A few years ago, those would be the best means of adjusting the way tyres heated up.

Tyres must come up to operating temperature in order for the car to work properly, and either they will or they won't. Nowadays, there are so many different tyre compounds available that there is usually one which will produce the desired effect.

Some corners are more important than others

With a current F1 car, it is virtually impossible to have a set-up suited to every corner on a given circuit. And, generally speaking, it is rare to drive a car in any category which is absolutely perfect in every respect! It is thus often necessary to compromise a couple of corners. This tricky decision depends on how the driver feels, but I sincerely believe that some corners are more important than others. I'm thinking mainly of those which lead onto long straights, where optimum speed is vital for overtaking. And you'll gain more time by being on the limit in a fast corner than in a slow one. Thus at some circuits I set the car up with one or two such critical corners in mind.

Control tyres

When testing or doing development work, you use what is known as a 'control tyre', i.e. an ordinary rubber compound, quite hard in nature. This is a good base for this type of circuit work, where you need to do a fairly high number of laps in stable conditions. No matter how often you pit and restart, you should always retain the same level of grip. If a tyre starts to go off, it becomes impossible to set up the car. Some tracks are too abrasive even for this type of tyre, and that makes meaningful testing difficult: you should never start out with tyres which are too soft or don't last. Tyre testing should be saved until the car itself has been properly balanced.

The influence of different driving styles

The way in which you drive naturally affects the way you set up your car. When Keke Rosberg and I were team-mates, our driving styles were so different that we adjusted what was effectively the same car in a radically different manner. But the main differences were mechanical rather than aerodynamic. I tend to have my car set a little stiffer at the front than it is at the rear. That gives me a touch of understeer and thus a car which is from time to time less efficient in mid-corner. On the other hand, I get more traction and more stability coming out of bends, which is always less wearing on the tyres, and my rears tend to last better. Keke, meanwhile, preferred the car soft at the front and stiff at the rear, as he preferred the car to be on edge at the entry to a corner. There are advantages to such a set-up at tight circuits like Monaco. That was one of the reasons he was always so at home on such tracks.

Test driving mentality

At the start of their career, young drivers don't just want to beat their rivals, they also want to stamp their authority on their team. They tend to have a preconceived idea about setting up cars, and when they're wrong they don't admit their mistake willingly. Getting into such a knot is the main problem of apprentice drivers. And it is also the difference between those who will make the grade and those who wi[ll] merely be average. When [it] comes to setting up a car, hon[esty] is all-important.

You can try anything on a ca[r]. I often suggest that I'd like t[o] try something, only for th[e] engineer to respond that [it] would be of no use for suc[h] and such a reason. I insist that [I] want to try it all the sam[e] because it's the only way to b[e] absolutely sure! And if I'[m] wrong, I admit as much: 'OK, it

Experience or lap times?

During practice, I always place more importance on the way the car feels than I do on lap times. Practice sessions are always awkward, and you must have your wits about you. With my experience, I know how to differentiate between lap times and reality: I might be half a second slower than a rival, yet happier than if I had been a tenth of a second faster, simply because I know exactly where there is scope for improvement. So it is a fundamental error to concern yourself exclusively with lap times. Analysis of the car has to come into it as well.

The problem arises with young drivers, as their team is likely to place more faith in their lap times than their feedback. The younger the driver, the more people place importance on lap times; the older they get the more experienced they become, and lap times become less important. For my part, I can forget about the stop-watch completely and say: 'I've done a quick time but take no notice. Change this or that and I think it'll be even better.' Either they'll believe you or they won't! They believe me...

doesn't work....' But at least I'm certain. This attitude is essential; it ensures the driver has no worries. It won't do to leave the pits thinking: 'Well, I should have tried this or that. It would have been better.' That just complicates matters. For testing purposes, you should never have any preconceptions, and you should try everything you can. And you must always be honest both with yourself and with the team.

Should you explain all ... or nothing?

I never drive my car without knowing its exact settings, and when I ask for something to be changed I always double-check to make sure that it's been done properly. On the other hand, at the start of his career a young driver might go out without being told exactly what his mechanic has altered, in order to sharpen his technical awareness and perhaps his objectivity. I remember when I ran a Renault engine in Formula 3. They never told me anything during engine development tests, whereas I had to recount all my observations in detail. This exercise is perhaps more logical for engine testing than it is for chassis development work.

Changes in chassis behaviour are more noticeable to the driver, and I think that he should be allowed to direct operations on this front. But whatever adjustments are made, and regardless of the type of car, a driver should never be stubborn while testing. Lack of objectivity can have a negative effect on the eventual outcome of his career.

RACING
ETIQUETTE

RACES AND RALLIES

It is important to differentiate between the two main motor sporting disciplines. We'll look firstly at circuit events. Here, three elements have to be considered: the circuit itself, the car, and the drivers, who are in direct competition. The object is to go as quickly as possible, while taking into account the constant presence of rivals, either alongside, just ahead or just behind.

Lap times, so crucial in qualifying, don't matter so much in the race. You are no longer looking to lap at the absolute limit, but rather to keep the opposition at bay and to develop sound tactics. The only thing that really matters is to be ahead of the rest!

This is quite different to rallying, where speed is the determining factor. But although you're racing against the clock it differs from racing in that competitors set off individually.

In rallying, you battle against the terrain, and your success is judged on the stop-watch. In racing, drivers thrash it out among themselves.

The direct confrontation you get on a race track demands a particular style of driving, which is worthy of lengthy consideration.

Hand-to-hand combat and wheel-to-wheel dicing constitute the principal differences between racing and rallying.

BEFORE THE START

■ The warm-up

For ten years or so now, both sprint (i.e. under two hours) and endurance races have been preceded by what is universally known as a 'warm-up'. This takes the form of a practice session on the morning of the race itself.

The warm-up allows you a final check on the way your car handles in full race trim. You aren't looking for the fastest possible lap, because it has no bearing on grid positions. It is simply an opportunity for driver and mechanics to make any last-minute adjustments.

The warm-up is important, because conditions mirror those in the race. If, after qualifying, you make a few alterations to the car, the warm-up permits you a brief opportunity to evaluate their worth and make necessary changes. It is the only chance you get to practise on race settings.

■ Start procedure

The running order of events leading up to the start of a circuit race makes for interesting reading.

– From the paddock, the competitors head for the assembly area, situated close to the circuit access point. If necessary, the clerk of the course will issue any last-minute instructions to drivers here.
– One by one, the drivers go out onto the circuit to complete a reconnaissance lap (or two, at the clerk of the course's discretion). They then take their places on the grid, as determined by their qualifying performance.
– The drivers then switch off their engines, and for around five

minutes the circuit is open to team managers, mechanics, journalists, photographers and so on.

– Then the start line marshal issues a series of boards, indicating the length of time before the start of the race (five minutes, three minutes, etc). At the two-minute board, everyone must clear the track, and the drivers should have fired up their engines. Anybody unable to do so should raise his hand as a warning both to officials and to other competitors.

– When the green flag is waved, drivers set off on a final warm-up lap (sometimes behind a pace car), maintaining grid order. They then line up on the grid, keeping engines running.

– When all cars are in position, an official standing at the back of the grid gives the signal to the start marshal.

– Finally, the race will be started either by the marshal waving the national flag, or via a lighting gantry. In the latter case, the drivers will be held for several seconds on a red light, and leave the grid as soon as the signal switches to green.

All drivers have a special moment for switching into concentration mode before the start of a race. For Ayrton Senna it seems to be the instant he dons his gloves...

■ The warm-up lap

When setting off on a warm-up lap, it is a common mistake to consider it as a simple exercise for bringing the engine up to temperature, warming tyres and putting heat into brake pads. In fact, the driver should already have clicked into racing mode. *The race begins on the warm-up lap.* It is worthwhile pushing the car a little bit, just to see how it reacts. If it results in a sideways moment or even a spin, no matter. Better that it should happen on the warm-up lap than at the start of the race itself.

■ Concentration

On race morning, the driver should concentrate hard as he counts down for the race. His concentration should intensify as the race approaches, so that it peaks at the time of the start.

Some drivers start to concentrate when the warm-up comes around, others just before the warm-up lap. This is down to the temperament of the individual. It is best to have reached the level of concentration demanded by the race by five or ten minutes before the start, at the latest. From then on, the driver should be left alone to concentrate his mind on the start and the first few corners. As a champion skier might envisage his two- or three-minute descent as he waits at the top of the mountain, so the driver must focus his attention on what might happen when the lights turn green, bearing in mind his grid position and who the other drivers around him might be. You should also imagine every precise detail of the lap to come, each bend, every gearchange, so that you're already racing in your mind when the event starts.

■ Hints on lining up on the grid

For better grip
All starting grids look the same. The cars line up two by two, with the pole position driver (having set the fastest practice time) holding the inside line for the first corner. Depending upon which side of the grid you find yourself, you will know whether that part of the circuit is in use during the

race itself.

If the first bend is a right-hander, the normal line down the previous straight will be to the left of the circuit. So the track will be cleaner on the left than it is on the right. A small point, but worth bearing in mind, although being on the 'wrong' side of the grid doesn't necessarily mean a bad start. That's why you might often see the pole position winner deviate from his line during the warm-up, in order to try and clear some of the dust and debris from where he will later start the race. This will afford him better grip.

Better positioning

Those drivers at the front of the grid will have their allocated positions rigorously enforced by the marshals. Those further back, on the other hand, won't be so closely watched, and can shift slightly to one side or the other of their 'slot'. It is simply competitive instinct coming into play. The only thing that matters is to make a better start than your rivals! So, if you can edge a little closer to the usual racing line, it is already a sign of your determination to make up a few places. If things don't go quite as planned in the opening moments of a race, you must act accordingly. But if a

driver is happy just to wait for openings if and when they happen, he'll miss out every time.

Simply being keen to pull a stroke – in this case getting past the car ahead of you on the grid – puts you in the right frame of mind for a good start. Such anticipation can only pay off providing you know exactly what you intend to do the moment the race gets under way.

Gerhard Berger's gaze sharpens, his eyes are fixed on the red lights ahead. The start is imminent...

HOW TO MAKE A GOOD START

The start is one of the most important moments of the race. A good one can immediately help you to overcome the handicap of a lowly grid position. A poor one might waste all your successful qualifying efforts in a second. It can have a bearing on the whole race, including the final outcome.

It is definitely the time at which there is the greatest risk of a collision. That is simply due to the fact that all the cars are so close to each other, and are released simultaneously to charge down towards the first corner.

Once the 30-second board has been shown, the start signal (whether it be flag or lights) is entirely at the discretion of the official responsible; these '30 seconds' are an approximation, and no driver should make the mistake of starting a mental countdown. As soon as that board has been shown, drivers should mentally be prepared for the start at any moment.

■ After the 30-second board

It's better not to engage first and slip the clutch too early, otherwise you'll run the risk of overheating it. There is a fine art to not being ready too soon! Sometimes, the start signal will be given later than anybody expects. The drivers sit, their eyes fixed on the lights or flag, and absolutely nothing happens!

This is normally simply because those cars at the back of the grid have not yet lined up correctly. A marshal will wave a green flag as soon as all cars are properly stationed: it's always a good idea to keep an eye on your mirrors to observe that signal. By knowing what's going on at the back of the

grid, you'll have a better idea about when the race is actually likely to start.

After the man with the board, all eyes turn to the start marshal.

There is a huge release of energy at the start, and just for a moment it is contained, inactive, on the grid. You must be ready to spring from the grid just as an athlete does from his starting blocks. The tension is such that nobody is safe from the possibility of making a big error. Sticking the car in third – or, worse, reverse! – instead of first can happen to the best of us. To avoid this possibility, it is worth releasing the clutch slightly and edging forward just a tiny fraction

The lights in the distance have changed to green. More than 20,000 bhp are unleashed at the same instant as 26 cars pounce together on the first corner!

to ensure that you are in first.

Once in gear, build up the revs to the right level: that doesn't mean to the absolute maximum, but rather to just below the point of peak torque. It is then best to maintain revs at that point, and not to blip the throttle as popular opinion would suggest you should at the start. Of course, if you were to do so and the start signal was then given at the moment you were accelerating, it would be perfect. But if it happened while your foot was coming up off the throttle, the

consequent slow getaway would count against you.

So it's best to keep the revs steady at the same level to eliminate this possibility; this also means you can take your eyes off the rev-counter, and study the start official and his lights or flag.

If you spend your time switching your gaze from the rev-counter to the start gantry, there is a reasonable chance that you will be taken by surprise.

As soon as the signal is given, there are three subtleties to master.

■ Slipping the clutch

Ensuring that the clutch slips neither too much nor too little demands a fine balance between two extremes.

Excess slip
This means that you are accelerating too hard while the clutch is still not fully released. The right foot is pressed down more than necessary, and very little, if any, power is getting through to the wheels.

Insufficient slip
The clutch is not allowed to slip sufficiently if you actuate it too quickly or too brutally, or if you fail to accelerate hard enough. In other words you lift your left foot too quickly and apply your right

too slowly. Thus the engine drops out of the power band, and while it may not actually stall (although that is a possibility) there will be a noticeable hiccup.

In the first instance – excess slip – power won't be distributed to the rear wheels, but will evaporate through the clutch itself and the car won't budge. In the second – insufficient slip – you have released the clutch too sharply and the car will only stagger off the line. That may not be too serious in the long term; the former may result in a cooked clutch.

There has therefore to be a compromise between these two extremes.

Following a tangle at the back of the grid (just visible in the first picture), the 1988 Portuguese Grand Prix had to be restarted. These two photos provide an interesting means of analysing the starting techniques of the front-runners.

In both cases, despite his position on a less clean part of the track, Alain Prost is up with Ayrton Senna, while Ivan Capelli has placed his March just behind the French driver's McLaren.

Elsewhere in the first picture, Berger has gone for the inside with his Ferrari, with Nigel Mansell's Williams tucked in just behind. Nelson Piquet's yellow Lotus can be seen on the opposite side of the track.

Curiously, on the second start, the Ferrari and the Lotus have swapped tactics, while all around them virtually nothing else has changed, as can be judged by the position of Mansell's Williams, which hasn't moved.

■. Finding the best grip

As soon as the clutch has stopped working, it has bitten, and your left foot will no longer be on the pedal. It is the right foot which will dictate whether or not the rear wheels spin, depending on how hard it hits the throttle; there is no longer any question of clutch slip.

If you accelerate too hard, the wheels will lay down streaks of rubber on the road and power disappears in a cloud of smoke; the car will either get away badly or stay put on the grid. Unlike the clutch, the driven wheels don't need to spin. The object is that they should be at the limit of adhesion; as soon as the wheels spin, they are no longer in firm contact with the ground. From a mechanical point of view, the problem is that the engine and transmission will receive a severe jolt as soon as the tyres regain full grip.

Everything is a matter of sensitivity. The driver wants to release the clutch quickly so that he has only his right foot to worry about. Vibrations in the chassis and the dial of the rev-counter will tell him if the engine is spinning too quickly, and the car will be slow moving off. If he can't see the rear wheels spinning in his mirrors, he will soon feel the back end of the car wavering gently. It's up to him to ease his pressure on the throttle in order to restore grip.

The right foot should be the embodiment of driving finesse. If the throttle pressure is right, it will feel the tyres bite the road fully. The wheels will then have their maximum grip, and all the power will be transmitted to the circuit.

A good start is one in which you don't see too much tyre smoke.

■ When should you take second?

This might seem too simple an issue to the man in the street, but you have to remember that at the start of a race you can't hear your engine at all. There are another 15 or 20 cars around you making just as much racket, if not more. In order to avoid making a mistake, it's best to look at the tachometer to avoid over-revving. But that isn't always possible, so it's best if you can actually detect when the engine hits peak power by sensation alone, and change up to second accordingly. Either way, it's best to change up too soon rather than too late in order to avoid, at best, hitting the rev-limiter, or, more seriously, doing long-term mechanical damage.

THE OPENING STAGES OF
THE RACE

Despite braking practically in the middle of the track, Nelson Piquet is snapped up by Ayrton Senna, who, from the outset, puts his first set of tyres to the test. The third-placed car, Benetton number 20, is not under threat and has opted for a more conventional line, something which cannot be said for the McLaren in fourth place, which is also planning on braking in the middle of the track.

It is often tricky to choose the best line when braking for the first corner. Generally, drivers go for the inside to avoid presenting their rivals with an easy overtaking opportunity. Here, Nigel Mansell, apparently off to a good start, controls the pack behind by braking in the middle of the track, sufficiently to the right to stop an opportunist from overtaking on the inside yet sufficiently to the left not to be handicapped by being on the slower line.

■ The first braking area

All cars arrive more slowly at the first braking area than they will have done during qualifying, when they had a longer run at it than they get from the starting grid. In theory, this difference in speed allows you to brake later. In reality, it is a matter of improvisation. It's a tricky thing to judge, as nobody has tried braking from this reduced speed during practice. So everybody is in the same boat, while there is the added problem of all the cars arriving in a bunch.

The further down the grid you go, the more this theory of 'late braking' is reversed, because the traffic jam is usually such that those at the back have in fact to brake much earlier than would normally be the case. By and large, those at the front brake later than usual, those in the middle at more or less the recognised braking point, and those at the back much earlier.

The nature of the first braking action in a race means that those who find a gap ahead into which they can dive will prosper. The general tendency is for drivers to aim for the inside of the corner to make it more difficult for others to pass. Coming into a right-hand bend the best place for an overtaking manoeuvre is on the right of the track. It is thus common to see drivers either in the middle of the track, or tight to the inside, to prevent their being overtaken. This of course freezes positions to an extent, and generally you'll come out of the corner in the same position you entered it.

However, if this tendency is exaggerated, it can create a blockage on the inside, and that opens up the normal racing line on the outside. Then it is a matter of opportunism and speed of reaction, which develops naturally as you gain experience of race starts. So the general pattern is for the cars at the front of the grid to take the inside line, and for those further back to take to the outside if no other route is available.

Braking for the first corner after the start is perhaps one of the most delicate moments in the course of a race. Cars are still dicing wheel to wheel and the occasional tangle cannot always be avoided.

While teams always try to plan against the unexpected, there always are and always will be unforeseen incidents in racing: a blown tyre which forces a driver to limp back to his pit, or a last-minute shower of rain when the car has been set up for the dry.

During braking for the next two or three corners, the tight grouping produced by the start gradually settles down, and normal overtaking practices gradually come into play.

■ The opening laps

During the first few laps, the driver must look to rediscover the rhythm and feelings that he had during qualifying, despite the close proximity of his rivals. And it isn't the presence of the other drivers that makes racing different to practice, but rather their increased aggression. Hence the importance of using all the landmarks to which you referred in practice to enable you to settle quickly into a rapid pace, in a slightly different environment to that of the previous couple of days.

OVERTAKING

A race can consist of several possible situations:

– there's nobody behind you, and you're putting pressure on the driver ahead;
– your rival is behind you, and you're on the defensive;
– you have drivers both in front of and behind you; you are trying to avoid being overtaken while simultaneously looking for a way past the car ahead.

■ Gaining a place

There is just one aim here: to overtake. In most circuit races, there is very little difference in performance between the various competitors. Overtaking a rival isn't simply a question of having more power than him. You can overtake if you have either:

– taken a corner better;
– exited a corner faster, and thus gained speed down the following straight;
– made better use of the brakes at the end of a straight.

No matter how you achieve it, overtaking isn't down to the successful accomplishment of just one feat, but rather a whole series of things. This is what makes circuit racing at the top level what it is; what makes it both appealing and challenging.

You have to prepare to overtake by studying your rival closely. Make a note of where he is slower than you, where he brakes slightly earlier, where he seems less at ease, or where he looks like he might make a mistake. His weak points constitute your strong points, and that should be the basis of your challenge. Always bear in mind, of course, the possibility of an opportunist manoeuvre which might present itself at any given moment. No driver is ever far from the possibility of making a mistake:

Overtaking by outbraking at the end of a straight is a classic way for a driver to move up a place. But the driver must be careful not to lose control in the middle of the braking zone with the rest of the field coming up fast behind!

This superb duel between Alessandro Nannini and Nelson Piquet took place during the 1988 San Marino Grand Prix. The top picture shows the Italian driver turning in earlier than the norm to keep his rival at bay. The bottom picture shows Piquet at the same spot checking on the margin between his Lotus and Nannini's Benetton. As can be seen by the slight locking of the Italian driver's wheel, Nannini is attacking hard, but Piquet has opted for a more conventional line through the corner.

THE PHENOMENON OF SLIPSTREAMING

The green car catches the black one progressively, until it enters its slipstream. From that moment, the green car will gain at a faster rate, as it faces less turbulence and thus penetrates the air more cleanly.

If the green car is travelling at the same speed as the black, and is outside the slipstream, it will gain no benefit. In order to profit from this phenomenon, it must either already be in the slipstream, or otherwise be travelling slightly faster in the first place in order to get into it.

The slipstream only takes up a small amount of space, and its benefits vary proportionally according to the speed of the car.

The driver will feel progressive acceleration throughout the slipstream area, and it is thus in his interests to stay in it as long as possible.

Having darted smartly out of the black car's slipstream, the green car will once again be faced with the same level of air turbulence as his rival, but the few mph he gained in his slipstream will allow him to seize the advantage. Timing is critical. If the green car waits too long, the driver risks losing any benefit as he will have to brake for the approaching corner. If he leaves the slipstream too early, he is unlikely to gain sufficient speed to enable him to pass.

It is worth noting that the green car is overtaking on the right. As there is no written rule about this in motor racing, there are two principal things the driver should bear in mind: the ideal line at the end of the straight, taking the subsequent corner into account; and the strength and direction of any prevailing wind. The driver of the black car is free to choose whichever side of the track he prefers, as he is ahead. So the driver of the green car may be allowed to overtake on the normal line, or he may be forced to use the less favoured side of the track. It is also best for the leading car to be on the opposite side to that from which the wind is blowing (in the diagram it blows from right to left), so that it doesn't offer extra shelter when the other pulls out to overtake. Naturally, these considerations may affect a driver's preferences, and that means he often has to work out the best compromise.

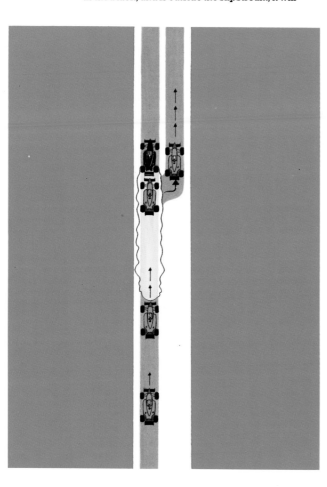

too long a slide, a slower exit speed from a corner or a missed gear (fifth instead of third) all present unforeseen overtaking opportunities upon which you should capitalise instantly.

Being alert and snatching every opportunity that comes your way is a fundamental necessity of racing. For if your rival's performance matches yours all the way around the circuit, there is logically no point at which you can overtake without risking a collision. Only an error, or a weakness at a certain spot, will allow you to nip past him.

If a rival is slower through a corner

You've watched attentively for several laps. Each time around, there is a spot where you are more at ease than your rival. So this is the basis for attack. That doesn't mean you will overtake him at that exact point; the speed differential probably wouldn't allow it. There are three possibilities.

On the next lap, you leave a slight gap between your two cars so that you don't enter the bend right behind him. If you stick to him too closely, that might force you to slow down, in which case you won't be able to profit from your extra speed. The size of the gap is difficult to evaluate. You don't want to give your rival too much breathing space, but enough to allow you to take the corner at your own pace, so that you'll be travelling faster than the other car at the exit, without it getting in your way. Your quicker exit speed will allow you to overtake down the next straight.

If this corner opens out onto a relatively long straight, you can gain an extra advantage by making use of his slipstream. This is an aerodynamic phenomenon which takes effect at around 60–75 mph, and thereafter becomes more significant the faster you go. To be in a slipstream you need to be tucked right in behind your rival, in a tiny area (only a few yards long) in which there is less air turbulence. It is your rival who cuts through the air just a few feet ahead of you, and this allows a gain of several mph in no time at all. In order to make full use of a slipstream, you have to be as close as possible to the other car. You know you are in the right place when you feel a drop in air turbulence, and – as a result – a slight increase in your own acceleration. But the manoeuvre demands expertise and not a little courage, bearing in mind that you may be only a few inches behind the other car at high

Each car in this procession benefits from the slipstream of the car in front. Note how they all follow the line adopted by the leading car in the group.

speed (135–155 mph).

Successful execution demands that you dart out at the last possible moment. At that point, you are back on an equal footing with your rival in terms of cutting through the air, but the speed you gained while protected from the turbulence will allow you to move past.

■ Attack under braking

Imagine that, having benefited from slipstreaming, you draw alongside your rival as you enter the next braking area. It would be ill advised to take any more risks than necessary to make such a manoeuvre a success. Just getting alongside, or perhaps half a length ahead of him, should suffice. There is no point in trying to do more. The idea is to brake a little later, either to get alongside or, better, half a nose cone's length in front. You then have right of way, bearing in mind that you should be on whichever side of the track constitutes the inside line for the next corner.

Your rival isn't obliged to give up without a fight. But if he tries to go with you around the outside of the bend, he runs the risk of going off the track. Quite often, young drivers, either through inexperience or impetuosity, try to get right past a rival in such circumstances, rather than being content simply to keep him covered.

If it is a long braking area, there is an added problem. Over 150 yards, for instance, you can make good use of the brakes over the first 100, and draw alongside your rival. But there is still the possibility of a counter-attack on his part, by braking and slowing down less over the last 50, in order to try and thwart your intentions.

There are two possible scenarios when you gain such a tiny advantage.

– You've overtaken on the way into the corner, but you are not on the ideal line, which allows your rival to anticipate the likely speed differential at the exit of the bend. He thus sticks to his normal line, taking the bend as though you weren't there, and in all probability repassing you down the next straight.
– You get to the corner ahead, but you've turned in too quickly, and it thus becomes paramount to fight for control rather than looking for a faster exit speed. That costs time, and your rival will exit the corner faster, easily powering past you down the straight.

These two instances suppose a classic confrontation between two closely matched rivals whose on-track conduct is correct. But in the

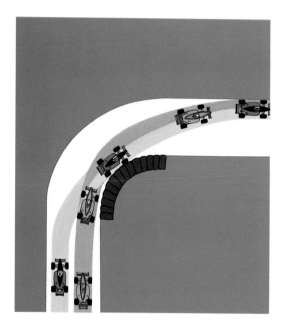

PREMATURE OUTBRAKING

The blue car tried to brake as late as possible in order to overtake the red one just before turning into the corner. Nevertheless, it had only drawn halfway alongside its rival. It didn't therefore have any right to take the ideal racing line, and thus the red car was fully entitled to turn in as usual, taking no notice of the blue car alongside.

If this happens at a circuit where normal safety measures are installed (large run-off areas and a rumble strip at the apex), the red car can take its line and leave the driver of the blue car with two options:

– to decelerate further by braking hard;
– if that isn't enough, he will be forced to put a wheel over the kerb on the inside in order to avoid a collision.

If, on the other hand, this takes place on a street circuit, where retaining walls and guard rails are close to the track, it is in the driver of the red car's own interests to acknowledge his rival's presence and allow him breathing space.

That doesn't mean he can't turn in ahead of the blue car, but he must do so less forcefully, while taking a slightly wider line than usual. In these circumstances, the attempted outbraking manoeuvre described will cost the blue car time, as it should at least have been fully alongside the red one before contemplating overtaking. Coming into the corner it is half a length behind; coming out, the gap will have grown to two lengths, the blue car's exit speed being reduced by its poor line through the bend.

IDEAL OUTBRAKING

The driver of the blue car has drawn alongside the red one on the inside line at the entry to the corner. It would be better to edge slightly further ahead, but in any case he has already thwarted his opponent by preventing him taking his usual racing line. The driver of the red car now has two alternatives:

– to allow the blue car to take the corner without blocking it, enabling it to complete its manoeuvre successfully;

– to stand his ground and take the corner on the outside line, which will be dirty and will therefore lack grip. When reaccelerating onto the straight, the blue car will gain the advantage.

In the first instance, if there is space, the blue car will drift back onto the normal line at the exit, forcing the red car either to back off or maybe even brake.

If the circuit is particularly cramped (with guard rails or concrete retaining walls), this would be ill advised as the red car would be trapped on the outside, with the consequent risk of a coming-together.

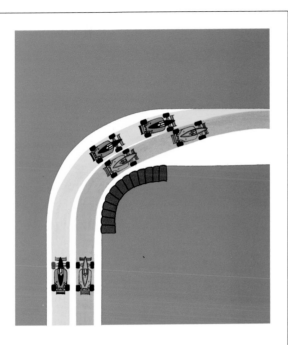

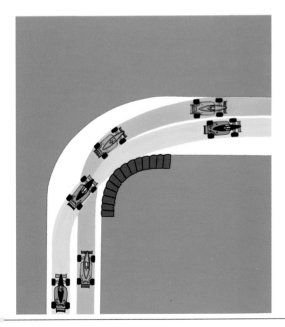

AN OVER-OPTIMISTIC CHALLENGE UNDER BRAKING

The driver of the blue car has overdone things. Not content simply to get alongside his rival, he has already shot past him.

He therefore risks entering the corner too quickly and not being able to turn in at the correct point, which will inevitably cause the car to skate wide onto the dirtier part of the track where there is less grip.

If the driver of the red car analyses the situation quickly, he will brake a little harder, let the blue car go by, and then take the normal racing line. And when they come onto the straight, his superior exit speed will carry him past the over-optimistic blue challenger.

heat of an extremely tight battle – as you always get in the closing laps of an event – there are other ways of reacting. When you have just scraped past a rival under braking, you generally realise fairly quickly that you have entered the bend too quickly, and thus rather than accelerating in mid-corner you are fighting for control. But by voluntarily breaking your own rhythm and not accelerating as you would normally you can force your rival to do likewise, and thus you should both enter the straight at the same pace.

Similarly, you can 'close the door' at the exit of the corner, just as the other car is shaping up to pass. Instead of staying on the line, you adopt a more aggressive attitude by staying in the centre of the track and making your rival's overtaking attempt all the more difficult. If his speed advantage is sufficient, he will overtake all the same; if not, he will attempt to get his own back in the next braking area, or on the following lap.

■ Pressure

As the laps accumulate, you might notice that the car you are following is braking as hard, is as fast down the straight and is coming out of corners every bit as quickly as you are yourself; simply, it is impossible to get past him. Logic suggests that you must therefore wait to seize upon the slightest error.

But the waiting game doesn't necessarily imply inactivity. You can wait by being extremely active, showing aggression, and convincing your rival that you have a couple of things up your sleeve even when you haven't. It's up to you to 'pressure' him into a mistake, as racing jargon has it.

There are a thousand and one means of pressurising an opponent. All are just as good: perhaps dive out late into a braking zone as if you were able to pass. Don't do it systematically, but just from time to time, at different corners, every other lap, always in a credible manner and with an element of surprise. In his mirrors, it is difficult for your quarry to tell the difference between a real passing attempt and a dummy. Maybe he'll be tempted to brake a little later, which implies the possibility of a mistake. And you didn't really have a chance, much less the intention, of passing...

So the more composed your rival seems to be at a given point, the better it is to make him believe that he's not really going that quickly, and that you are looking to pass.

On the other hand, if there is a spot where you really are quicker, it's best not to give the game away. Delay

playing your ace in order to take him by surprise.

When you aren't intending to pass, it's best not to stay too long to his side, but to get back behind him quickly before the turn-in point, so that you stay on the racing line. Then you are best placed to make the most of any subsequent error, whether in the middle or at the exit of a corner.

Pressure can equally stem from constant harassment. You are no quicker than your rival, but you are as quick as him. And you must let him know it at every available opportunity. Through every corner, down every straight, you should be close enough to fill his mirrors. Your presence alone will put him under heavy pressure.

This form of attack is no less

Nelson Piquet, under pressure from Michele Alboreto, brakes in the middle of the track. As soon as the following bend is reached, the Italian can go for the ideal line on the left.

Constant use of rear-view mirrors is vital to fend off attacks during a race. Riccardo Patrese, one of the most difficult drivers to overtake in a fair and square tussle, knows how important they can be.

important for its psychological nature.

But it goes without saying that the experience of the drivers concerned will influence the outcome: the result will not be the same if an experienced driver is hassled by a newcomer as it might were the situation reversed.

■ Holding position

Defence depends entirely upon your rear-view mirrors. That is an essential point. Mirrors aren't there just so that you don't block a faster car – when you're heading for the pits, for instance. They must be positioned so that you can deduce at a glance what your rival is up to. Where is he quicker than you? And where is he slower? Don't forget, you should check your mirrors feverishly at the same points every lap in order to get a precise picture. Generally, the exit of a slow corner is a good reference point, as the gap is likely to be smaller than it is in a fast bend, where it is accentuated by the higher speeds.

In principle, there is no point trying to make ground at places

The marshals' blue flags are used to promote understanding between drivers, contributing to the proper running of the race.

where you are already quite comfortable; you should be under no threat there, and you'd be risking an error. But at points where your rival is quicker concentration and application are of prime importance if you are to go more quickly.

How should you defend yourself from some of the aforementioned challenges?

In a corner

It's best to tackle corners with maximum commitment if you know your rival is a shade faster there. All well and good if you succeed; if not, you must recognise your own personal limit, which you should not overstep on any account, as that will only cost you time.

On the straight

If your rival is in your slipstream, there is not a great deal you can do. From time to time, gentle zig-zagging down the straight might break the tow, by forcing the other car to confront the air turbulence with which you must contend.

In the braking area

It's imperative to brake as late as possible to prevent your rival drawing alongside. If you just manage it, to the point that you reckon you are only marginally ahead, you should stick to your normal line without taking his presence into consideration. If there is a kerb on the inside (as is the case at 80 per cent of circuits), you shouldn't hesitate to take the normal line. It will be your rival's responsibility to brake, or take to the inside kerb, to avoid you. Obviously, on street circuits, where the track is bordered directly by guard rails or walls – and there is no run-off area – you must take your rival's position into consideration. In either case, you shouldn't allow yourself to be duped. Depending on how far advanced a race is, you should strengthen your resolve accordingly, as described below.

In the opening laps
The running order isn't yet established, and drivers tend to close the door to make overtaking more difficult.

After four or five laps
The race is now in full swing. Fair play should prevail, and you should stick to the normal line.

In the closing stages
As the end of the race draws close, it is accepted that drivers have the right to defend more vigorously. Everything is down to the temperament of the driver on the defensive. At best, that means driving in the middle of the road in order to force one's rival outside the boundaries of an ideal overtaking position. At worst, it means closing the door by slamming firmly over to the far right of the road into a right-hander. In that instance, the only overtaking route is around the outside, which is always more difficult.

It goes without saying that such actions are only acceptable in the final few laps. It would be intolerable to carry on like that for the whole length of an event. And it has to be admitted that such actions can elicit a similarly aggressive response, particularly when one competitor is noticeably quicker than his adversaries in the closing stages.

In the middle of the pack
Finally, one of the most difficult situations in which to hold down a position is when several drivers are running together. It isn't easy to defend yourself while simultaneously trying to get by the car ahead. If you protect your position too forcibly, you risk losing ground to the man you are chasing. Conversely, if you attack

without sufficient thought, the following drivers will more than likely put you under increased pressure. It's difficult to strike a balance. Only common sense and sound tactics can help. So, if you are slightly faster than the car in front, but aren't certain that you can pass cleanly without losing time, don't try anything at the start of a race. If you stick with him until mid-race, and eke out a gap to the following cars, then you can have a go at dealing with him on his own...

In the middle of the pack, it is important not only to defend one's own position but also to maintain constant pressure on the car in front. This is one of the most difficult aspects of racing to master.

Alain Prost's comments

The difference between practice and the race

The problems you have finding a suitable set-up to achieve the best qualifying lap are vastly different from those posed by the race. In practice, for instance, I might set a very fast time because the car is particularly good through two or three slow corners. In the race, on the other hand, I might still be quick through those corners, but if I'm not fast enough down the straight or through quicker bends then I'm going to be overtaken by my rivals, and frustrated by my car's handling. You often see cars which are quick in qualifying but which fail to match that performance come the race. Thus a car might set fastest lap in a race without ever being in front of certain others, simply because it is too slow down the straight or handles badly through a particular part of the circuit.

That's exactly what happened to me during the French Grand Prix a few years ago, on the old, long circuit at Le Castellet. I certainly had one of the fastest cars that day, although I was short of outright speed down the Mistral Straight, which made overtaking difficult. Furthermore, and I'm not sure why, I was ill at ease through the quick right-hander leading onto that straight. That handicap was too much to overcome, even though the car was actually very effective over the course of a lap. But that one corner was one of the most – if not the most – important points on the circuit.

How not to be overtaken

Sometimes you opt for an aerodynamic set-up that is particularly effective on the main straight. So, after a qualifying session in which I have gained pole position, I take off as much aerodynamic downforce as possible in order to be quick down the main straight, prepared to compromise a little in certain corners, but not so much that I can be overtaken. For that reason, you obviously don't want to take this idea too far!

Holding station at the start

At the start, I think that everyone should hold station. It's dangerous enough as it is! With a few exceptions (when a mechanical breakage, of which there are a decreasing number, has been to blame), all the serious start line pile-ups have been due to collisions between two cars.

The more you weave at the start, the more chance you have of collecting a rival. And if I was to do that, there's no reason why the driver behind shouldn't do it to me at the next race.... Resultant contact can have a snowball effect, and the end result is that you no longer have a car fit to race!

Should you close the door?

In racing, I think that closing the door is practically a matter of education. It is possible to do it once or twice, when the driver feels that all is well but he's been delayed either by missing a gear or being held up by a back-marker. In such circumstances, I concede that closing the door is permissible. As it is when you're battling hard for victory over the course of the final few laps. But closing the door from start to finish, as some drivers do, is simply not acceptable. If I was ever to win a race by blocking throughout, I'd gain no satisfaction from it and certainly wouldn't be proud of my actions.

Dicing in a race

Each time I'm leading a race and the driver behind challenges me, I can never be sure whether he's making a serious bid or not, and that always puts me under pressure. When you're behind, on the other hand, it's best to time any move to perfection, and not to give the car ahead advance warning about what you're planning, so as to keep it a surprise.

The smaller the gap between two cars or two drivers, the more you have to prepare your move. It can sometimes take 30 or 40 laps before taking all the relevant information on board; it's a bit like a game of cat and mouse. You have to be completely aware of your adversary's every move; but if he should miss a shift from third to fourth, you must be ready to pounce in an instant! That is a sign that he is getting tired, or that his gearbox has started to play up and that he will make the same mistake again. Maybe it would be a good idea to put pressure on at the same place next time around, in an effort to make him repeat the error. Following a rival closely is also the best way of monitoring how his rear tyres are lasting. When they are loaded up, you can judge their wear rate by observing a dark patch which is clearly visible on the tread.

The most difficult passing manoeuvre is that when you are quicker than your rival through corners, but slower down the straight. You can spend a whole race tucked in behind this sort of problem! The difference in speed quite often leads to accidents: you have to make your move carefully, preferably under braking at the end of the longest straight. In every overtaking manoeuvre, there are two attitudes you must consider: that of the driver on the defensive, and that of the challenger.

So if there is a coming-together, responsibility has to be apportioned both ways, even if one driver carries 99 per cent of the blame. Usually, if two drivers enter a corner side by side, logic says that the man on the inside has the advantage. But in the past we've seen countless accidents resulting from the refusal to give way of the driver on the outside. Often, the driver trying to pass is blamed. But in reality, in order for an overtaking manoeuvre to be a success, I think that there has to be a good loser as well as a good winner.

Spins

There are numerous ways of provoking a spin (or several of them!) by losing control of your car. It can happen under braking, when there is too much bias towards the rear, or it can result from going too fast into a corner, producing excessive oversteer. It also occurs when you accelerate out of a corner in the wet. Whatever the circumstances, the driver should always react in the same way: as soon as he senses a loss of control, he should brake hard and simultaneously keep the revs up to prevent stalling. The second objective is to try and keep the car on the circuit, rather than the grass. In the latter instance, the lack of grip will cause an already out-of-control car to pick up speed.

Going off the track...

Unfortunately, this is very much a part of the sport, so we have to talk about it! One of the most awkward cases is when the front wheels lose grip, and the car goes straight on. Mechanical failure apart, this happens when you leave the ideal racing line, and find yourself on the 'dirty' part of the track (covered in gravel, rubber particles or dust). Generally, you can't even throw the car into a spin, and in all honesty when you know you're going to hit something there's nothing more you can do about it! At the last moment, sometimes you lift your feet from the pedals, despite the lack of space, and try to make yourself as small as possible inside the car. You also release the wheel, just before the impact, in order to protect your wrists.

When the car goes sideways (oversteer), you should do everything possible to regain control, but only up to a certain point, beyond which a serious accident becomes a possibility, as has sometimes happened. At the end of its slide, the car can suddenly regain traction and spear straight into the barriers on either side of the circuit. You see situations like this at Indianapolis. Most of the fatal accidents occur when drivers try so hard to regain control that the car suddenly grips and heads in the other direction, straight into the concrete wall. There, statistics prove that the drivers who come off best are those who, upon losing control, are happy to brake as hard as possible. The car often then follows the radius of the corner, and sometimes even finishes up on the inside, safely at the bottom of the famous American track.

Instinct

A driver cannot be taught to identify the moment at which he should decide that it is better to spin off rather than hit the barriers at a bad angle. It is purely a matter of instinct. In spite of which, there are a few objective points to consider. Is it a fast or a slow corner? Is there a run-off area or are the barriers close up? Is the surface smooth or bumpy? It might not seem important, but a car going sideways on a bumpy circuit might fly off in the other direction, completely out of balance. And while you might easily bring the car to a halt in a slow corner, a fast curve will present quite a different problem!

Flag signals

Whenever I see a yellow flag (danger: be prepared to stop), it always worries me a little. If I see two or three of them, it concerns me even more. In fact the more I see, the more I worry! There again, it's true that marshals often seem agitated, as though there has been a major catastrophe, when in reality there has been nothing of the sort. I'm thinking for instance of a car which has just pulled up on the straight, bringing out the yellow flags. In that case, I'd take no notice. But when I can't see what's going on, and I don't know what to expect, I'm extremely careful, and I slow right down, sometimes almost to a halt.

As far as waved blue flags are concerned, the rules are unclear. Officially, it means another car is trying to pass. But that can apply to a titanic scrap for third place just as easily as it can to the leader coming up to lap the man in 12th.... There is no difference in the signal, which is a shame, for it can be ambiguous.

Physical fitness

I've always played a lot of sport for pleasure (football, tennis, cycling and running). When I started in F1 (with McLaren in 1980), I never did any specific muscular exercise. The best way to do that was simply by driving the car, particularly where the neck was concerned. But I've always tried to have a healthy way of life. Then, when I rejoined McLaren in 1984, I thought that, faced with Niki Lauda, it would be best to change my approach, as we had the same car, the same team and identical chances of becoming World Champion! I therefore adopted a fitness programme like his so that there would be nothing between us. At first it wasn't obvious, but I began to feel much better, and since that time I've always felt in peak condition and have never been tired after a Grand Prix.

I've also played a lot more sport than I used to! Plenty of golf during the season (for relaxation and concentration), running (minimum 4 km, maximum 12–15 km for at least 300 days a year), cycling (indoor in the winter, on the road in summer), rowing (arms and forearms) and also sauna work.

As for diet, I eat meat only once a week, otherwise sticking to raw vegetables, fish, milk products and salads. I don't smoke and I only have a glass of wine occasionally. During my time with Renault, my heart-rate was 65 beats per minute. Today, it's down to 48 and my stamina equates to that of a downhill skier in the heat of competition.

Communication with the pits

Ever since I started in racing, I've always wanted to know the gap between myself and my two closest rivals: the one in front and the one behind. In addition to this vital information, my pit board also tells me my position, the number of laps left to run and how much fuel I theoretically have left. Sometimes I ask which drivers are holding the top four or five places. The radio link is handy during testing, but in a race I only use it if it's a matter of urgency, and I don't like to receive messages which I may not pick up clearly. That would distract me. When I need to make an unexpected pit stop, for instance to change tyres, I signal my intention by putting a hand on my helmet as I pass by the pits one lap before stopping.

The element of risk in motor racing

There are some drivers who think: 'This corner should be flat ... so I'll take it flat.' No matter that their car isn't set up correctly. Having said that, you notice that they try, but realise that it isn't on, so they don't do it. And that's only right. If it was simply a matter of courage, and taking as many risks as possible every so often, motor racing wouldn't exist! You have to prove you have various qualities in competition: the ability to set the car up, courage, motivation and shrewdness. They are all connected, because one day you will need to work harder at sorting the car, the next you will have to call upon your personal strengths to plan your challenge. Generally, those who function on bravery alone, and who take the most risks, are not the best drivers.

Courage, motivation, aggression

I don't relate courage and motivation. Courage is something you either have or you don't, and it doesn't really change. Well, perhaps just a little according to your results or your age...

Motivation, on the other hand, can be fine one moment, and disappear completely the next. There are highs and lows, according to circumstances. The better the car a driver has, the greater his chance of success, and in that case he has no problem motivating himself.

Now, taking a fast corner flat out, but perhaps not every lap because it is that difficult, demands both courage and motivation. But I think that all the top drivers have the same degree of bravery, apart from perhaps two or three, who try things that aren't really on.... It isn't up to me to decide whether that's a merit or a flaw. That's simply the way they are. Me, I prefer to take a corner flat out because I've set the car up properly, rather than getting a buzz from doing so in an ill-handling car, even if that has happened to me.

This sequence was taken during the 1983 Dutch Grand Prix at Zandvoort. Alain Prost explains: 'Overtaking Nelson Piquet here shouldn't have presented the slightest problem. It was a classical attack and Nelson, with whom I have since spoken about the incident, admits he was beaten. But Zandvoort is a circuit where there can be lots of sand around the track and, as soon as you come off line, the track can be very slippery. Furthermore, the surface on the inside of this particular corner was bumpy.... I remember my car rising at the rear over a bump and a wheel locking. The car went slightly sideways and, since Nelson was very close, I hit him with my front-left wheel. That wasn't so drastic, but I went on to lose grip at the front. When that happened, all four wheels locked and I took the Brabham off.

'To make matters worse, I punctured his front-right tyre with my front-left wing – which can be spotted on the photos – which left Nelson even less capable of reacting and regaining control of his car.

'This slow-speed incident took place at around 100–120 km/h (60–75 mph), Nelson ending up in the wall of tyres without too much damage. I was able to continue, but my front wing later collapsed going into a fast corner. With no grip, I went straight off! I remember looking for Nelson in my mirrors, thinking he was still mobile and about to overtake me again. It really should have been a straightforward, incident-free overtaking manoeuvre and I was very upset that it ended the way it did.'

Five years later, the two super-drivers – who have six world drivers' titles between them – again confronted each other during the San Marino GP. That day, however, the two cars were visibly not in the same league and Alain was able to pass with ease.

HOW TO BECOME A CHAMPION

Above and beyond the different aspects of driving technique, setting up a car and race tactics, several questions still remain. When and where should you start? How can you learn to drive a racing car properly? How and why do you become a champion? Obviously, there is more than one answer, but there are several firm conclusions to be drawn from what has happened in French motor sport over the past two decades.

There are generally two hurdles an aspiring professional driver must tackle successfully. The first is arduous, but it is one most manage to conquer. It relates directly to natural driving ability and hard results: either you know how to race or you don't. Such criteria can be judged objectively.

The second is appreciably more demanding. It is here that the majority fail, and most of their illusions are shattered. It is difficult to define what qualities a driver requires, as it depends more on subjective matters, such as mental approach and morale. A driver can either cope with life's ups and downs – or he can't.

■ When and where to start

One of the first problems an aspiring young driver will face is the minimum age for obtaining a driving licence. From a physical viewpoint, it is obviously possible to handle a racing car before you are 18. There is no shortage of examples, and in countries where drivers may obtain a licence one year earlier young debutants are no more or less out of their depth than they are elsewhere. For many years the first step has been to start out in motor cycle competition, which teaches you a number of important things: racing lines; how to use an engine and gearbox; aggression and racing in a group. A whole generation of motor cyclists passed successfully from two wheels to four: John Surtees (former motor cycling World Champion, and World Champion with the Ferrari F1 team in 1964), the late Mike Hailwood (former motor cycling World Champion and later an accomplished F1 racer), Jean-Pierre Beltoise and the late Patrick Depailler, to mention just a few.

More recently, karting has taken over as the breeding ground, which follows the motor cycling idea that if you can't race a car you should do the next best thing. And karting technology has advanced to such a level that the most powerful of them will now lap at speeds somewhere between those of Formula Renault/Formula Ford and Formula 3. So, a young driver who has shone in kart racing will inevitably be faster in a car than an equally gifted rival who waited until he had a driving licence before starting out in racing. That's a shame in so far as it means future champions really have to make their debut in a kart, and therefore have to start very young. There has been no shortage of gifted young drivers whose lack of maturity has drained them completely as soon as they faced any real problems. This syndrome has certainly snuffed out natural talents before they have had a chance to flourish fully.

François Cevert was 23 when he entered his first season of racing, while Jacques Laffite didn't get going until two years later, at the age of 25. Neither came from karting or any other motorised sport, but it didn't stand in the way of their exceptional careers.

In fact the only recommendation as far as getting started is concerned is to enrol at a top racing school, of which there are many in France (as there are in Britain). Twenty years ago, the Magny-Cours school was the only one, but now there are so many that the choice can be confusing. For comparison purposes, the best thing is to study how each school's top graduates have progressed over the years. The best pupil from a good school generally wins races, and maybe even a championship, within his first couple of years of racing. That shows that he is gifted, but also that the school has enabled him to make full use of his ability. On the other hand, some drivers vanish as quickly as they first appeared...

■ Racing schools

A single-seater racing school has several objectives. First of all it's fun, so different is a single-seater to an everyday saloon car. Then you learn a whole host of things that you were never taught when you first learnt to drive. Tuition is naturally focused on the particular techniques of race driving, but you can also adapt it for less aggressive daily use. As far as racing is concerned, such schools allow anybody to find out

their true potential without going to great expense. If you are among the top 20 pupils at a school which receives 250 each year, you ought to get started straight away. At the very least, you'll enjoy success as a gifted amateur, although there have been F1 drivers, exceptions rather than the rule, who didn't score too highly back in their racing school days. Not going to a school would seem to limit your chances of success from the outset. But that won't stop you from racing, nor from deriving a great deal of pleasure from the sport.

In France a system has been developed over the years which has seen many drivers progress smoothly along a well-oiled conveyor belt from the junior levels of the sport to Grand Prix racing. Each racing school has an annual competition to select its pupil of the year, which allows many young drivers to fulfil their wildest dreams. Winning will launch you into the sport with a fully sponsored drive in one of the junior formulae, a prize that can lead to greater things.

Remembering that there will inevitably be a great many disappointed pupils, some of whom will respond to their 'failure' more philosophically than others, it might be worth pointing out that the management of any well-run racing school will do everything possible to ensure that the prize-winner is the most deserving pupil. Its reputation, the level of success achieved by its protégé and its commercial prospects depend directly upon its making the right choice. It is in the instructors' interests to pick out and develop the star pupils.

■ What breeds success?

It would be pretentious to offer a concrete solution to a question drivers have long been asking themselves in vain. There isn't a simple answer.

For my part, I believe that success at the highest level of the sport owes much to a driver's mental approach, his natural ability only coming into play afterwards. An exceptional champion like Alain Prost has an impeccable mental approach to his racing, even if all you see is his considerable talent at the wheel. Seen from the edge of the track, everything is unflustered, flowing and efficient, yet at the same time he will be on his way to setting the fastest qualifying lap! But the truth

is that his natural talent is enhanced by a tremendous will to overcome any problems and an enormous desire to win at all costs.

In 1976, during his first season in single-seaters, he won 12 out of 13 races. He was French champion by a mile and his immediate future held no worries. It was only in the last race that he suffered a mechanical failure, and he was massively angry. Even today he regrets not having maintained a 100 per cent record! Having the feel for a car and being able to drive it quickly isn't such a rare thing. But to suffer all sorts of trials and tribulations, disappointments and uncertainties, and all the while retain your motivation, suggests that you have the strength of character that will eventually make the difference.

During an international F3 race in Britain, I had a good starting position among 40 or so aspiring champions. Among them were three who would become World Champion: James Hunt (with McLaren in 1976), Jody Scheckter (Ferrari, 1979) and Alan Jones (Williams, 1980). Although Jody Scheckter had already shown his potential, the other two had done nothing to indicate they were in any way special, either that day or any other. It would have been ridiculous to suggest that they might race in F1! Several years later, they were developing as Grand Prix drivers when many of those who used to beat them were nowhere to be seen...

Simply, their mental fortitude allowed them to succeed in challenges where others had failed.

To recap, the ideal situation is to have mental strength coupled with natural talent: the two most obvious examples of the last decade have been Alain Prost and Ayrton Senna. The second possibility is to be a slightly less gifted driver, but to have sufficient will to win to overcome that initial drawback. You could classify Niki Lauda thus, his early career being largely undistinguished as he struggled to qualify with 'bought' drives, before eventually becoming one of the greatest drivers of all time. Finally there are the magnificently talented young drivers who disappear after a mercurial start to their career, the memory of what they have achieved to be recalled only through the pages of old magazines. In order not to ramble on at length, I won't name any of them.

Before concluding these reflections, I'd like to recall an astonishing competition debut that I remember well from having been a direct rival: that of Jacques Laffite. At 25 he raced in F3 having finished second in the racing school competition at Magny-Cours. At 26 he dropped into Formula France (then the equivalent of Formula Renault) where he did nothing special. At 27, still competing in Formula France, he won his first race. At 28, in his fourth year of single-seater racing, he was French Formula Renault champion. Who would think, after that mediocre start, that Jacques Laffite would be the second-greatest French driver of all time, in the wake of Alain Prost?

Alain Prost's comments

'This Formula Renault Martini was my first single-seater. With it, I won 12 out of 13 races, took pole 11 times and set 11 fastest laps...'

The best way of getting started in racing

I have always thought that the best way to get started is to enrol at a single-seater racing school. Nowadays, many young drivers try their hand before going to one of the schools, whether it be karting, Renault 5 racing or any of the other one-make series. It's certainly an advantage to enrol at a school with previous experience to your credit, and karting is the best bet. When I hear it said that karting is good preparation for F1, that's no exaggeration! Karting can teach you everything you need to succeed at a school. It's a positive step just to have a steering wheel in your hands, before you are old enough to hold a road licence. The ambience and the competitive mentality help develop your character, the importance of which shouldn't be underestimated when a young driver faces up to the final stages of a racing school competition.

My first steps in motor sport

I was 17 when I started karting, and within a few seasons I had graduated to World Championship level, where I met for the first time drivers such as Riccardo Patrese, Eddie Cheever and the late Elio de Angelis. You can't compare driving an F1 car with driving a kart, but it provided a fantastic education for me, and the driving standards were just as good as they were in Formula Renault at that time.

It was obvious that this experience helped enormously when I attended the Winfield school at Le Castellet, and gave me an important edge over equally gifted rivals who had no similar experience. So I deliberately kept a low profile during the two months which preceded the final. I didn't want to draw attention to myself, nor show the opposition what the likely target would be!

For instance, I noticed that by exiting wide from a rapid left-hander, and by going over the rumble strip, I gained between 100 and 200 revs down the following straight. I discovered that by chance, but I made sure that I didn't let anybody else know, and saved it for the final. And it was only the day before the final that I finally charged my batteries fully and went at my maximum pace, which was about two seconds a lap quicker than my rivals!

Biggest problem for a young driver, and...

The biggest difficulty facing a young driver is to go quickly without making mistakes. I remember in karting, I used to get within millimetres of the marker tyres, almost brushing them. The mistake came when I touched them. I always sought such precision and accuracy of judgement, and it pays off today. In Formula Renault, I made mistakes from time to time, notably in qualifying, but I wouldn't slip up in the same way during the race.

'Even if it might be considered by some to be a "sedentary" sport, motor racing can take a lot out of the body, and proper physical training is essential.'

...best advice

It seems to me that analysis is hugely important. We have already seen that it is imperative to make as few mistakes as possible, but a driver will inevitably make some. It is essential then to analyse them and find out why they happened. Everything should be treated as a lesson, so that you are always making progress.

It is impossible to advise a young driver in specific 'do this, do that' fashion. There are too many variables, such as the type of car, the driver's character and his mental approach. Analysis, however, is simple: 'I lost a race for this reason; I made a mistake because of that; the car was badly set up. Why?'

I think that the desire to analyse has been one of my strengths, and I always think like that nowadays. For me, analysis is also a matter of not losing your motivation, nor letting a problem lessen your resolve, nor becoming fatalistic.

The best advice I can give to any beginner is to analyse everything he is doing.

PHYSICAL PREPARATION

Along with most motor sports, racing has often been accused of not being a sport at all. To the uninitiated, the car seems to count for more than the driver. Of course, it has a part to play. However, motor sports are distinguishable from most other sports; in the former, the engine creates the movement, whereas in the latter that is down to the athlete. There is a big difference between creating a movement and controlling that emanating from an outside force.

Thus physical preparation for motor sport is quite specific. Drawing an analogy with the car, if that requires bodywork, then the driver must have a physical framework suitably adapted to driving it.

The engine could be compared to the cardio-vascular system, the heart's job being to dispense blood through the arteries and around the body in order to instil the necessary energy.

One of the characteristics of motor sport is that it accelerates the heart-rate significantly. Tests on an active F1 driver have shown that it can rise to 190 beats per minute, and that it rarely drops beneath 120 in a race, the difference depending upon the stress level, a difficult corner or an overtaking manoeuvre, for example, prompting a rise.

The results of this analysis lead us to suggest a few physical activities which aim to reduce the driver's basic heart-rate. These are feats of endurance, and are most effective if you don't overdo it: you should not exceed 120 beats per minute.

The onboard computer is like the brain and nervous system, which enable you to control your speed to best effect:

– by 'feeling' the road through the intermediary of the body;
– by observing the best lines;
– by memorising all the reference points around the circuit;
– by overcoming the stress of speed, danger and the unexpected.

These qualities, pushed to the limit, are the signs of a true champion. They can be developed and maintained.

Roland Krzentowski
Sports Physician
Clinique du Sport

The racing driver is an athlete who practises his art while glued to his seat and whose movement is not controlled by his limbs.

Motor racing is not a sport of physical power, but one of control and sensitivity, of stamina and endurance.

The driver's body is subjected to considerable loads by acceleration, braking, cornering and the vibrations and heat of the car, all of which exert considerable muscular strain on the upper limbs, shoulders, neck and torso.

Alongside basic cardio-respiratory preparation, which comes from regular running or cycling, there are other useful pursuits, such as skiing (with reference to the perception of speed and the need to judge corners), golf and tennis (concentration, self-control and tactics).

However, any physical effort which reinforces the muscles directly affected by driving will prove advantageous when it comes to fighting off muscular fatigue and tension.

Here is a series of simple exercises, which don't demand special equipment and can be practised for a few minutes every day at any time, in any place.

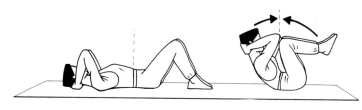

Bring your elbows up to the knees, touch your right knee with your left elbow, then the left knee with your right elbow. Don't forget to breathe (figure 1).

■ The torso

The chest should be considered as a solid block, for two reasons:

1 – The upper limbs, crucial to driving, need a sound base to be effective when pressed down by the shoulders.
2 – The spinal column should be firmly supported to reduce the effect of all the bumps and jolts.

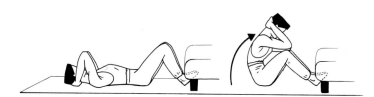

With knees bent, lie on your back and wedge your feet tight (under a bed for example). Slowly draw yourself up in a rolling movement until you touch your knees with your elbows, remembering to breathe. Take a deep breath in this final position, then unroll the spine as you breathe out until you are back in the original position (figure 2).

a) abdominal movements
Back flat on the floor, hands crossed behind the neck, knees bent; while breathing out, sit up so that your elbows meet your knees, and then return to the horizontal starting position while breathing in (two lots of 20 – see also diagrams 1, 2 and 3).

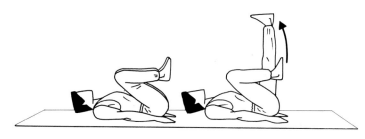

On your back, with your knees against your chest and arms laid alongside the body, lift up each leg alternately and keep it stretched vertically while holding the other knee against the chest (figure 3).

188

b) back and neck movements

Sitting position; firstly find the ideal position, then rise to your full height, and lean forward with your back 'locked' in position, always keeping your body fully stretched (see also diagrams 4, 5 and 6).

■ Arms, forearms, wrists, shoulders

The upper limbs should be kept solid in order to avoid cramp when tensed on the steering wheel.

a) Arms

Biceps: flex your elbow with a 5 kg weight in each hand (five lots of 20). Triceps: press-ups with hands together.

b) Forearms, wrists

Sitting down, forearms on thighs, flex your wrists with a 5 kg weight in each hand, palms facing upwards (four lots of 20). Stretching: back of the hands facing upwards, flex your wrists with a 4 kg weight in each hand (four lots of 20).

c) Shoulders

A 2 kg weight in each hand, raise your outstretched arms to the horizontal (two lots of 20), then repeat with your arms by your side (two lots of 20).

d) Shoulders, pectorals, triceps

Press-ups, arms apart.

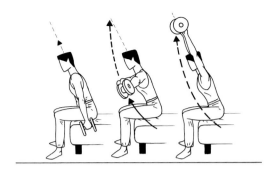

With a 1.5 kg weight in each hand, bring your arms up above your head in a semi-circular movement. Keep your arms in the axis of your body at all times (2 × 20 movements – figure 4).

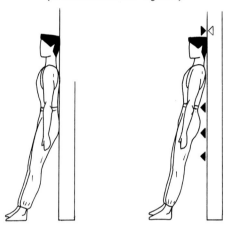

Stand with your back against a wall, your feet about 18 inches away from it. Move your hips forward to bring your back off the wall, leaving only the head to support your weight (1 × 20 movements – figure 5).

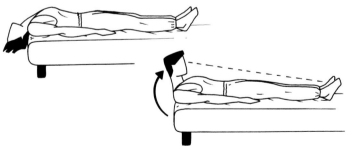

A useful neck exercise is to lie on your back on a bed, your head just off the edge. Bring your head up and forward so that you can see your feet, then let your head drop back to the original position again (1 × 20 movements – figure 6).

Pierre Ribette
Physiotherapist
Clinique du Sport

Despite three World Formula 1 titles and an all-time record of 43 Grand Prix wins to his name (following the 1990 British GP), Alain Prost has never lost his characteristic spontaneous smile and modesty.

ALAIN PROST'S RECORD

Born 24 February 1955 in Lorette, near St Chamond in the Loire Valley.

1972 Karting debut.
1973 2nd in French karting championship.
1974 French and European karting champion.
1975 French karting champion and Elf scholarship winner, Winfield racing school, Le Castellet.
1976 Formula Renault champion with 12 wins, 11 pole positions and 11 fastest laps.
1977 European Formula Renault champion with 6 wins.
1978 French Formula 3 champion and Formula 2 debut.
1979 French and European Formula 3 champion with 9 wins, including Monaco.
1980 F1 debut with McLaren. 15th in World Championship.
1981 5th in World Championship with Renault. 3 wins.
1982 4th in World Championship with Renault. 2 wins.
1983 2nd in World Championship with Renault. 4 wins.
1984 Return to McLaren. 2nd in World Championship. 7 wins.
1985 World Champion with McLaren. 5 wins.
1986 World Champion with McLaren. 4 wins.
1987 4th in World Championship with McLaren. 3 wins.
1988 2nd in World Championship with McLaren. 7 wins.
1989 World Champion with McLaren. 4 wins.
1990 Joined Ferrari. 4 wins in first 8 races.

Three World Championship titles, 20 pole positions, 32 fastest laps and an all-time record of Grand Prix victories (43 after the 1990 British Grand Prix).

PIERRE-FRANÇOIS ROUSSELOT'S RECORD

Born 8 May 1948 in Casablanca, Morocco.

1967 Saloon car debut.

1968 Runner-up Magny-Cours racing school scholarship.

1969–1973 105 single-seater races in Formula Renault (35) and Formula 3 (70). European F3 champion in 1971, beating Patrick Depailler.

1975–1989 11 participations in the Le Mans 24 Hours (1st French team home in 1988 with an Argo-Cosworth). 8 participations in World Endurance Championship events (2nd at Paul Ricard in 1977 with a Toj-Cosworth; 1st at Monza and Mugello, 1982, with a BMW M1).

1973–1977 Instructor, Magny-Cours racing school.

1978–1983 Director, Magny-Cours racing school.

1974–1988 Journalist-test driver for *AutoHebdo* and later *L'Automobile*. Has tested several Formula 1 cars: Martini-Cosworth, Ligier-Matra, Ligier-Cosworth and Renault; plus Constructors' Championship-winning Williams-Cosworth in 1981 and World Championship-winning Brabham-BMW in 1983.

1989 Director of France Prototeam, a contender in the World Sports-Prototype Championship.

Pierre-François Rousselot pictured putting the Renault RE50 Formula 1 car – 850 bhp and only 540 kg! – through its paces.